CUSTOMER RELATIONSHIP MANAGEMENT

Making Hard Decisions with Soft Numbers

Jon Anton
Purdue University

CONTRIBUTING AUTHORS
Purdue University:
Jodie E. Monger
Richard A. Feinberg
Rick Widdows
Limburg University:
Ko de Ruyter

Prentice Hall
Upper Saddle River, New Jersey 07458

Library of Congress Cataloging-in-Publication Data

Anton, Jon.
    Customer relationship management / by Jon Anton.
      p.   cm.
    Includes bibliographical references and index.
    ISBN 0–13–438474–1
    1. Customer relations—Management—Statistical models.
  2. Customer relations—Management—Case studies.   I. Title.
HF5415.5.A58   1995
658.8′12—dc20   95–33737
                                            CIP

Editorial/Production Supervision and Interior Design: *Walsh Associates*
Director of Production and Manufacturing: *Bruce Johnson*
Managing Editor: *Mary Carnis*
Acquisitions Editor: *Elizabeth Sugg*
Manufacturing Buyer: *Ed O'Dougherty*
Marketing Manager: *Frank Mortimer, Jr.*
Cover Design: *Bruce Kenselaar*
Figure Art: *Suzanne Vierling*
Production Liaison: *Carol Lavis*
Editorial Assistant: *Kahdijah Bell*

 © 1996 by Prentice-Hall, Inc.
A Simon & Schuster Company
Upper Saddle River, New Jersey 07458

Printed in the United States of America

10 9 8 7 6 5 4

ISBN 0-13-438474-1

Prentice-Hall International (UK) Limited, *London*
Prentice-Hall of Australia Pty. Limited, *Sydney*
Prentice-Hall Canada Inc., *Toronto*
Prentice-Hall Hispanoamericana, S.A., *Mexico*
Prentice-Hall of India Private Limited, *New Delhi*
Prentice-Hall of Japan, Inc., *Tokyo*
Simon & Schuster Asia Pte. Ltd., *Singapore*
Editora Prentice-Hall do Brasil, Ltda., *Rio de Janeiro*

Contents

Preface

PURPOSE

In today's highly competitive global commercial market, products come and products go with life cycles becoming ever shorter. For companies large and small, the most important real asset with measurable long-term value is loyal, one-to-one customer relationships. Strangely enough, this very important and eminently tangible asset does not show up on the company's balance sheet, nor is it listed in the typical annual report to the stockholders. Why doesn't the company's financial system account for this critical asset? The answer, simply, is most companies don't know how. Primarily for that reason, we felt compelled to write this book demonstrating the cost-effective techniques we have used to assist company managers in accomplishing strategic customer relationship management.

A recent study completed by Purdue University researchers showed that 87 percent of the Fortune 500 companies surveyed had the words "customer relationships," or "customer satisfaction," in their corporate mission statement, yet only 18 percent had implemented a method for measuring this elusive asset. We have developed the materials for this book from our experience in working with companies that are quantifying their performance in achieving customer satisfaction.

It is our purpose to document practical and cost-effective methods of customer relationship management through proven qualitative and quantitative techniques. Because of the nature of measuring people's attitudes and opinions, we have borrowed the term "fuzzy logic" from modern computer science, which also must deal with less than dichotomous variables—not zero nor one, or neither yes nor no. In the business world, where customer experiences are continuous and perception perpetually changing, we fuzzy thinkers hold that "truth" itself constantly changes in the "eyes of the buying customer." Our goal in this book is to give the nontechnical corporate manager the tools to better retain customers by making "hard decisions" with the "soft numbers" used to measure customer relationships.

SCOPE

The vast majority of today's professionals managing companies have no formal experience in the qualitative and quantitative methods of customer relationship management. In planning our book we focused on two audiences of readers, namely:

1. Those that find themselves caught up in the current wave of corporate interest in customer relationships, yet have no formal training or experience in managing this important asset.
2. Business students at both the graduate and undergraduate levels who will soon be joining companies that are struggling to redefine themselves as being customer-focused.

For this reason we begin with the business importance of fostering long-term customer relationships to gain market share, and then demonstrate the qualitative and quantitative methods we have used to measure a company's performance as judged by the customer. We then focus on demonstrating to the reader five specific case studies where measurement techniques were used to make hard business decisions with the soft numbers of customer response.

We have sought in this book to minimize the theoretical "stuff" and focus instead on real-world examples and practical applications. Since it has been our experience that many "wanna-be" customer relationship managers don't know enough statistics to process their own surveys properly, we spend one complete chapter on processing a very real survey. Chapter 7 uses SPSS software examples, a sample database of survey responses, and a step-by-step analysis of survey results.

Most importantly, after you have "experienced" this book, its our hope that you will be completely comfortable designing and implementing a measurement system that will enhance your company's ability to manage customer relationships.

About the Authors

DR. JON ANTON is with the Department of Consumer Sciences at Purdue University and a member of the Center for Customer-Driven Quality. He has assisted over 200 companies in improving their customer service strategy/delivery by implementing measurement systems through information technology. Dr. Anton received a Doctorate of Science and a Master of Science from Harvard University, a Masters from the University of Connecticut, and a Bachelor of Science from the University of Notre Dame. He also completed a three-summer intensive Executive Education program at the Graduate School of Business at Stanford University.

DR. RICHARD A. FEINBERG is a professor and Head of the Department of Consumer Sciences and Retailing at Purdue University. Before coming to Purdue, he taught in the psychology departments of Juniata College and Ohio State University. Dr. Feinberg has his Masters of Science from the State University of New York, and a Ph.D. in consumer psychology from the University of Oklahoma.

DR. JODIE E. MONGER is the Manager of Research for the Center for Customer-Driven Quality at Purdue University. She has assisted numerous companies to quantify their current levels of customer satisfaction. She received her Ph.D. and Masters of Science from Purdue University, and has a Bachelor of Science from Juniata College. Dr. Monger's special career focus has been on quantitative methods of customer relationship management.

DR. KO DE RUYTER is a member of the faculty of Economics and Business Administration in the Department of Marketing and Market Research at the University of Limburg in Maastricht, The Netherlands. He received his Ph.D. from the University of Twente in Holland. Dr. de Ruyter has focused on corporate complaint management strategies and has published two books on this topic. He has also assisted companies in Europe to improve the information quality of customer relationship reporting systems.

DR. RICHARD WIDDOWS is a professor of Consumer Economics in the Department of Consumer Sciences and Retailing at Purdue University. Dr. Widdows has published research papers in consumer affairs in a number of journals, including *Mobius, The Journal of Consumer Affairs,* and the *Journal of Retailing.* He is a regular contributor to leading professional meetings in consumer affairs. He holds a Ph.D. and Masters Degree in Economics from the University of Missouri at Columbia, and an honors Bachelor of Arts from the University of Leeds in the United Kingdom.

1

Customer Relationship Management

INTRODUCTION

In today's fast moving and highly competitive market, products come and products go. For companies large and small, the most important real asset with measurable long-term value is loyal, one-to-one customer relationships. Strangely enough, this very important asset does not show up on any company's balance sheet. Why doesn't the company's financial system account for this critical asset? We have found that the primary reason is simply that there seems to be no accepted method in place to measure it.

If a company lost 10 percent of its inventory to theft, swift action would be taken to turn the tide. If a company is losing 10 percent of its customers to competitors, no one might even notice it. Some companies have been experiencing the slow and quiet erosion of this major asset, the customer. If it were real property or inventory, accountants would be measuring the loss and taking swift action. Frequently, most of these companies do not specifically manage their customer relationships, so this asset can just slip away unnoticed until it's too late.

In this chapter we will stress the importance of establishing a recognizable method of measuring the health of customer relationships. We recognize that by its very nature, the system you adopt will have a certain amount of "fuzzy logic," and therefore, the theme of this book is to show managers how to deal with the "less than exact" customer relationship measurement tools. For this reason the subtitle of our book is "making hard decisions with soft numbers."

RELATIONSHIPS HAVE BECOME VERY IMPORTANT

In today's increasingly competitive environment, customer relationship management is critical to corporate success. Delivering high quality service and achieving high customer satisfaction has been closely linked to profits, cost savings, and market share (Sager, 1994). With this focus on the customer, leading companies today are overhauling their traditional financial-only measurements of corporate performance, and seeking new metrics (both internal and external) that include customers' perceptions and expectations.

Financial measurements are straightforward mainly because there is a "unit of measure," namely, the dollar. The relationship measurement techniques discussed in this book transform qualitative—that is, "soft"—numbers into statistically sound numbers and indexes for decision makers. We call our analysis of the results "fuzzy logic," in that it is not an exact science, yet it is plenty accurate for management purposes. We recognize that there is a complete engineering science called fuzzy logic, however we have simply adopted the word and not the methodology.

According to Peter Drucker, "The business of business is getting and keeping customers" (Drucker, 1979). Therefore, to retain customers we must have a stronger focus on measuring and managing the individual customer relationships. In short, all companies are in the service business, that is, satisfying customer needs, which, therefore, must be measured and tracked.

Slowly but surely, corporate America is learning that the customer is king and the king is demanding. He or she wants one-stop shopping from multidivisional companies, easy-to-get status reports on what's happening with his or her order, superefficient transactions over the telephone, and more and more and more. The old paradigm was price, quality, and service. The new paradigm is price, quality, service, speed, convenience, value, solutions. . . , yes, all of them!

FUZZY LOGIC 1.1

> *"The key is getting closer to our customers and making it easier for them to do business with us."*

We're all having to rethink our focus from "bottom line" to the customer's every need and want. The paradigm shift all companies are trying to make is to provide more internal and external customer relationship focus.

The more superlatives the better, whether you're making trucks, tractors, or serving hamburgers and/or lemonade.

People usually think of a customer relationship as a continuous activity, an intangible that cannot be measured. Thus the first challenge in creating a customer-focused culture at your company is defining a customer relationship in a way that it can be measured and therefore managed.

Even though most people would identify the work they perform as a customer "service," they would be hard pressed to define what service means. Think of the various ways the word "service" is used in our society: customer service, financial service, consulting service, military service, medical service, lip service, religious service, secret service, repair service, information service, postal service, stud service, creative service, social service, civil service, to name only a few—very confusing, to say the least.

Companies want to stand out from the pack by offering extraordinary service that makes it hard for customers to look elsewhere. Since services cannot be inventoried, per se, the mindset for developing a competitive customer service strategy must be different.

In this age of product likeness, in which the market fails to perceive any profound difference between products or companies and any product advantage today is copied by the competition tomorrow, quality customer relationship management is the only thing that can place one company head and shoulders above the rest.

INFORMATION ENABLES ONE-TO-ONE RELATIONSHIPS

FUZZY LOGIC 1.2

> *"Modern information technology makes possible these close, 'customerized' relationships that lock in customers for life by substantially enhancing the customer-perceived value of the product/service."*

Most companies today are underutilizing information technology, and therefore "missing the boat." Today's winners are capitalizing on available information technology to meet the customer challenges facing their organizations, and as a result, the winners are better and faster and cheaper and newer than their less technology-nimble competitors.

In today's "nanosecond nineties," successful corporations are doing what was once considered impossible. They are increasing customer satisfaction, shortening process cycle and response times, reducing costs, and developing innovative new products and services, and all at the same time!

"All cars are extremely well-made today, so the area of service becomes the only remaining distinguishing factor," said Frank Kery, manager of the customer-support center for Ford Motor's North American Automotive Operations (Williamson, 1993). Improving customer service through information technology is one of the hot issues for information systems executives, according to *Computerworld* (Panepinto, 1994).

With the advent of the many information technology tools available for the toll-free inbound customer service call center, companies have a virtually limitless "toolbox" for customer relationship measurement and management. These include, but are not limited to, such relationship enhancement activities as one-on-one consultative selling, customer education, complaint management, database target marketing, and real-time satisfaction monitoring.

Chief information officers (CIOs) are digging into such familiar applications as electronic data interchange (EDI), imaging, groupware, and workflow software to speed up the processing of customer transactions. The winners of the new millennium will be those who can develop a culture that allows them to move faster, communicate more clearly, and involve everyone in a focused effort to serve ever more demanding customers.

"With 'service added' an increasingly important strategy, all sales are fast becoming 'system sales.' All transactions must be looked at as relationship-building opportunities" (Reichheld, 1993). American CEOs must recognize that sustained profitability comes from retaining customers through increased productivity and information technology, not just low wages. Only major education and training investments will create the knowledge workers with the skills to employ new technologies to "wow" customers, while improving productivity and justifying their higher wages. In customer relationship management, the people are a major factor in achieving success; pay them to think, not to be busy. Motivate them to bring their brains and hearts to work and not just their bodies.

All CEOs have the awesome task of ultimately making a profit for their company to survive. Therefore, telling a CEO that "you must focus on your customers" through the use of expensive information technology may fall on deaf ears if we cannot show that these investments will come back in terms of revenue, market share, and profits.

A study by the University of Louisville in Kentucky showed that early adopters of information technology used to enhance customer relationships—companies such as Citicorp—won more market share and increased profits as a direct result of these investments. However, Citicorp showed no productivity gains because the company did not reduce costs or labor (Betts, 1993).

FUZZY LOGIC 1.3

> *"Be careful not to use information technology to simply 'pave the cow paths' of traditional business processes that affect customer relationships."*

Customer-oriented information technology systems can empower an employee to manage successful interactions with customers—the thousands of daily "moments of truth" that occur between customers and companies every day. To achieve this, systems must be easy to use, intuitively designed, and quick to change. Most importantly, these systems must provide the customer's requested information almost instantaneously. One of the most important attributes driving customer satisfaction is the availability of accurate information on a timely basis.

Customer relationship pressures have forced an increasing number of organizations to reassess the way they work, simplifying complex business processes to reduce cost and improve efficiency and enhance customer-driven quality. Technology can play a leading role in this area, and can rekindle interest in systems/software to monitor, track, and better manage customer relationships.

MARKETPLACE FORCES IN ACTION

In Figure 1–1 we can see the marketplace forces in action. The war of business has shifted onto a new battleground. In the 1960s, marketing was the watchword for achieving competitive advantage. In the 1970s, manufacturing became the hot topic, and in the 1980s, quality. Now competition has arrived at the fourth corporate battleground—customer relationships.

Within companies, building customer loyalty has become everybody's responsibility. Trite stuff, but really crucial. In the past, we have built fat, risk-adverse structures that are filled with too many undertrained, undermotivated employees.

If you think losing a customer or two here and there means little, or that you're better off without those nitpicking, piddling complaints, then consider this: Should just one customer a day who usually spends $100 per week stop doing business with your company, you will lose $1.9 million in annual

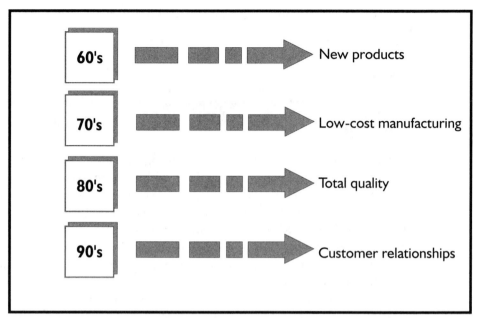

Figure 1–1.   Marketplace forces in action.

revenues, and this does not include the additional potential loss due to the bad word of mouth from dissatisfied customers (Harris, 1991).

More and more, when it comes to customer relationship management, every CEO needs to consider not "if it ain't broke, don't fix it," but instead consider "if it ain't been fixed lately, it will most probably break soon" (Mackay, 1993). Typically, about one-third of your customers leave you for reasons you cannot really control. Tragically, however, according to a recent AMA study, the remaining two-thirds leave because you provide poor customer service (Dutka, 1993).

As importantly, as can be seen in Figure 1–2, when customers are asked, "Why did you change products or suppliers?", a whopping 68 percent reply "I had a problem with customer service!" In other words, we terminate most customer relationships by not focusing on managing that relationship.

With a nod to his company's competitors, Phil Rathburn, director of customer service at Dow Chemical, said, "We all are producing high-quality chemicals and plastics, we are all essentially selling at competitive price levels, and we all offer similar kinds of attributes. How then, can a company inspire loyalty among its customers?" (Williamson, 1993). The answer is "develop unique services and manage your customer relationships closely through information technology."

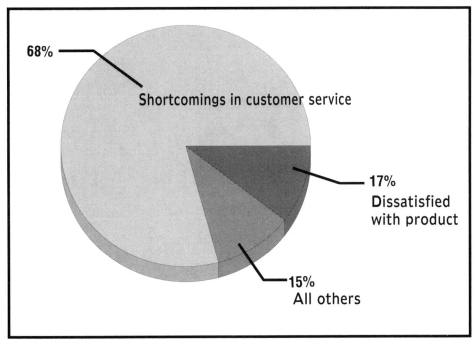

Figure 1–2. Why do customers leave companies?

Fortune magazine effectively characterizes service strategy as "knowing exactly which customers (companies) you want to serve and figuring out exactly what kind of service will loosen customers' purse strings" (Tschohl, 1993).

WHAT CUSTOMERS WANT FROM YOU

What customers want most is a real relationship with the companies whose products and services they buy. As can be seen from Figure 1–3, the customer's needs are simple, but the corporate challenge of delivering this kind of one-to-one relationship is major.

To encourage customer relationship management, Corning Glass's CEO encourages sales representatives to make "penpals" of the purchasing agents they deal with, using information technology such as MCI Mail to discuss golf scores, vacations, and, not quite incidentally, the availability of Corning's new catalog. "The key to us is using information technology to build customer relationships," he explained at a recent conference (Shrednick, 1995).

* Responsiveness

* Knowledgeable people

* Promptness

* Promises kept

* Understanding

* Security

* Followup

* No surprises

* Accuracy

* Communication

* Accessibility

* One-to-one interaction

Figure 1–3.   Customers want a relationship.

WHAT IS CUSTOMER RELATIONSHIP MANAGEMENT?

Figure 1–4 shows the many elements that are included in customer relationships, and also emphasizes the complexity of managing this important asset of your company.

In this book we will focus mainly on describing simple and cost-effective ways to measure and manage each relationship with the goal of discovering continuous improvement ideas as guided by the customers in each specific relationship, that is, being customer-driven.

The typical customer relationship cycle includes at least the steps depicted in Figure 1–5.

"The chain of events that leads to customer satisfaction begins with design decisions and runs through marketing, all of manufacturing and field sales, and culminates in after-sales support," stated John A. Young, the former CEO of Hewlett-Packard at a high-tech conference (Clark, 1993).

Listening to customers and seeing their perspectives, providing reliable,

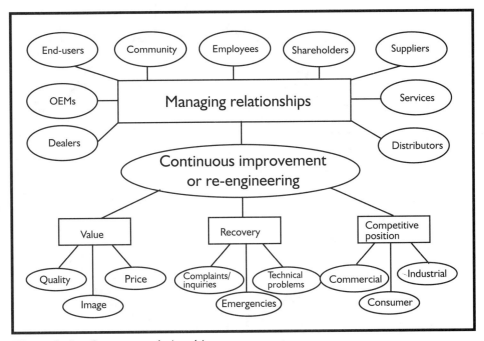

Figure 1–4. Customer relationship management.

excellent service, having the information technology installed to make sure that the service strategy happens, being able to recover on the fly when you do make a mistake, delivering service above and beyond the expected, developing a spirit of teamwork, listening to employee perspectives, and having management that leads by example are all keys to success.

The customer relationship phases that should be measured and consequently managed to achieve success are shown in Figure 1–6.

This shows the typical company as an integration of multifunctional, multidiscipline workgroups, each with a purpose and a product/service to provide to the customer. Figure 1–6 sets in motion our investigation of which processes are ripe for improvement or re-engineering due to their importance and impact upon the external customer.

The steps of managing customer relationships, differentiating customers, defining expectations, and measuring quality all deal with effectiveness. They answer the question "Is the organization doing the right thing right for the customer?" When companies embark on improving an activity, most look at changing how they do what they do (their processes). This is an area of great opportunity, but the wrong place to start.

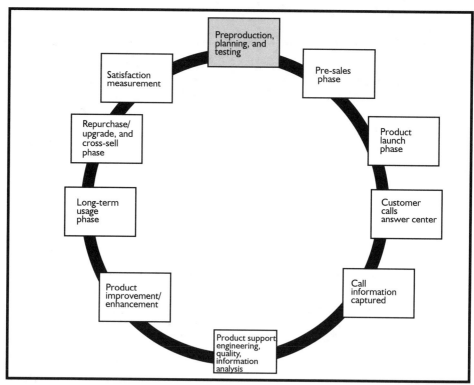

Figure 1–5. Customer relationships.

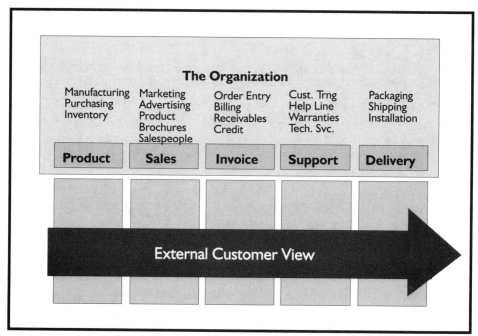

Figure 1–6. Processes that affect the customer.

"First let's get effective, then let's get efficient."

A company can create a wonderfully efficient, error-free process but still produce something its customers don't want. The fact is that customers generally don't care how a company does its work. This focus on internal activity encourages producer-centered thinking.

BOTTOM-LINE RETURN ON LONG-TERM CUSTOMER RELATIONSHIPS

FUZZY LOGIC 1.5

"Across a wide range of business, the pattern is the same: The longer a company keeps a customer, the more money it stands to make."

"When you build a plant, it starts depreciating the day it opens. The well-served customer, on the other hand, is an appreciating asset" (McGarvey, 1995). In Figure 1–7, you can see the real magic of customer retention, and the real reason for you to focus on managing your customer relationships. When you can increase customer loyalty, a beneficial "flywheel" kicks in, powered by:

- Increased purchases of the existing product
- Cross-purchases of your other products
- Price premium due to appreciation of your added-value services
- Reduced operating cost because of familiarity with your service system
- Positive word-of-mouth in terms of referring other customers to your company

Remember, it costs on average five times more to replace an existing customer with a new one.

AT&T did a six-year study comparing their market share to customer-perceived value and found the results shown in Figure 1–8 (Lian, 1994).

Figure 1–8 shows a period of time during which AT&T was re-engineered completely to make the customer "number one." Notice how exactly market share parallels customer-perceived value. Research has shown that

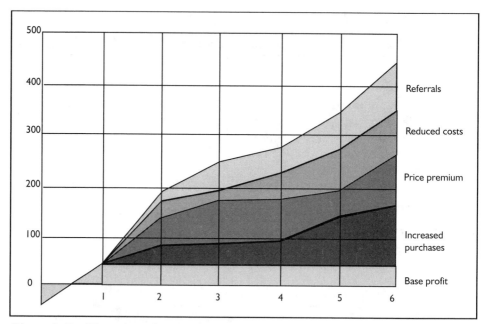

Figure 1–7. The value of one customer.

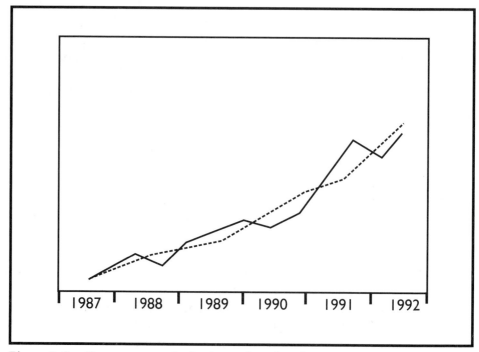

Figure 1–8. Customer-perceived value and market share.

customer-perceived value and satisfaction are excellent leading predictors of next year's revenue, market share, and profits.

In 1992 WordPerfect increased market share by 7 percent without introducing a single new product. Only their outstanding customer service with unlimited free support on their inbound 800 number could claim credit for this unparalleled achievement (Tehrani, 1993).

"A drop in market share soon follows any perceivable decline in customer-perceived product value. This loss of share outweighs any short-term saving managers achieve through cost-cutting" (Tehrani, 1993).

Arthur D. Little, Inc. has discovered a basic truth concerning service quality, one that is found in every industry it has studied: Improved service quality results in a consistent pattern of increased market share and revenues. According to ADL, customers are willing to pay a reasonable price for the value added by quality service (Hamilton-Smith, 1993).

Consider, for example, the results of a study, called "Profit Impact of Marketing Strategy," by the Strategic Planning Institute. After following 2,600 businesses, the PIMS study found that the most important single factor affecting performance is service quality relative to that of the competition. In other words, there was a direct relationship between customer satisfaction and profitability (Gale, 1992).

The PIMS study showed that companies ranking high on relative perceived service quality had an average return on investment (ROI) 15 percent higher than low-ranked companies. The leaders also found that they could charge on average 9 percent more for their products while increasing market share 6 percent. Companies can WOW customers while maintaining good balance sheets.

By the techniques discussed in this book, it is our intention to demonstrate to the reader how to uncover continuous improvement opportunities in people, processes, or technology as depicted in Figure 1–9.

LESSONS LEARNED

✔ To survive in this competitive global economy, companies large and small must become more customer-focused.

✔ In order to become customer-focused, companies must set in place a measurement system that includes the voice of the customer.

✔ The customer information system, by its very nature of monitoring

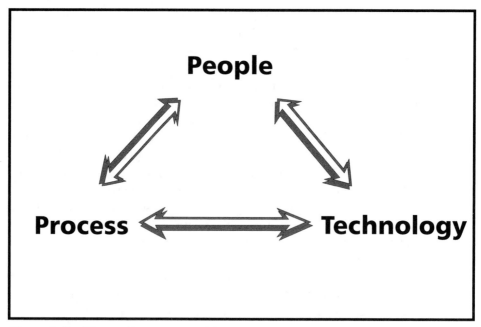

Figure 1–9. Uncovering opportunities.

the attitudes and expectations of human beings, will be made up mostly of what we have come to know as "soft" numbers, also called soft metrics.

✔ Because customer relationship measurements begin with qualitative inputs, we use the term "fuzzy logic" to describe the method of making hard decisions with soft numbers.

✔ Every study performed to date indicates that companies that focus on the customer become the industry leaders in both profits and market share.

2

Management Requires Measurement

CORPORATE MEASUREMENT SYSTEMS

"If you can't measure it," goes the old cliché, "you can't manage it." In fact, if you don't measure it, most managers seem unable to pay attention to it.

FUZZY LOGIC 2.1

> *"Only measure what you plan to improve."*

Measurement is management's way of saying it cares. It is helpful to look at how business measures reveal cultural values. Measurements are usually developed with some bias. Producer-focused organizations heavily favor financial information. They commonly used four measures—namely, profitability, productivity, specification-based quality, and schedules—to illustrate their priorities. Here are the drawbacks:

1. These measures might not be integrated or organized by product, and therefore it is difficult to determine how changes in one variable affect other variables.
2. Management activity is focused on improving processes that might have little relationship to customer interests or customer-perceived value.

With modern information technology tools, we have the capacity to analyze and evaluate almost anything, but too often we are measuring the wrong things, gathering the wrong data, and then interpreting it into the wrong conclusions. Witness the roller-coaster mentality of many companies in terms of *rightsizing* and *downsizing* one year, only to be short-handed the next.

Currently, the primary measurement systems used to manage a company are completely devoid of any report on the "voice of the customer." Top management thrives on being financially focused, and today's MBA graduates pride themselves on being able to interpret the company's "financials" and make hard decisions based upon "hard numbers."

The financial-focus equation shown in Figure 2–1 explains our current obsession with "bottom line" profit, and why we spend so much time budgeting for next year and monitoring sales reports, production volumes, and the like. For financially focused companies, the main management tools are budgets, combined with income statements and the balance sheets. To emphasize this focus, these companies have monthly "dollar day" meetings to discuss and interpret the financial reports.

Continuing on with this focus, let's observe how executives currently manage, for example, the invoice processing system. As shown in Figure 2–2, the financially focused manager would conclude that the purpose of this system is to "collect money owed for products sold or services rendered." Logi-

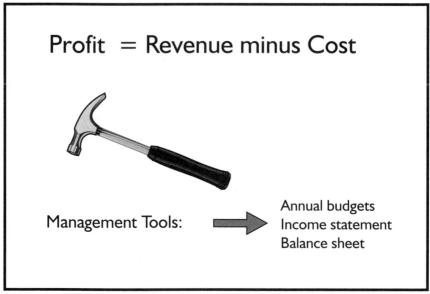

Figure 2–1. The financial-focus equation.

Collect money for products sold

Figure 2–2. Company's purpose of invoice processing system.

cally, as shown in Figure 2–3, the manner in which this process is currently managed is reporting on the accounts receivable. The average age of all receivables is also a critical cash flow metric to watch when managing this process.

By contrast, the customer-focus equation is shown in Figure 2–4, and here the emphasis is on what today's customer considers important, namely **value.** If we're going to be customer-driven in managing our customer relationships, we must learn to use new measurement tools. The most common tools and techniques are customer surveys, critical incident monitoring, advisory panels, and focus groups. These are discussed in Chapter 3, with case studies described in Chapter 10.

If we revisit the invoice processing system from the customer's point of view, we see in Figure 2–5 that the customer has different needs and/or expectations regarding receiving an invoice.

FUZZY LOGIC 2.2

"In order to include the voice of the customer in our management style, we must include measurements that are indicative of customer satisfaction."

Figure 2–3. Therefore, we measure . . .

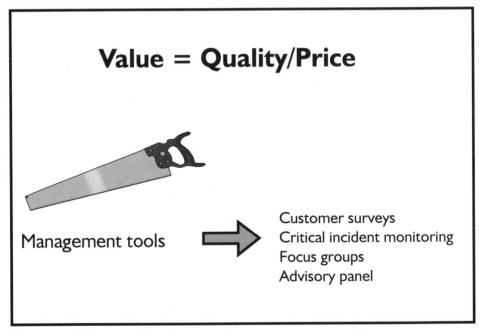

Figure 2–4. The customer-focus equation.

Figure 2–5. Customer's perception of invoice processing system.

As shown in Figure 2–6, there are several internal metrics that could give us important management information regarding customer dissatisfiers: (1) frequency of billing errors, (2) problems resolved on first call, and (3) timeliness of bill payment. The customer satisfaction results must drive an internal corporate behavior that we can measure, change, and improve. In Chapter 4 we will focus on how to use these internal metrics as an ongoing measure of external customer-perceived value and satisfaction.

In today's atmosphere of international competition, the only way a company can distinguish itself in the marketplace is by adding customer-driven value to its basic service. That means offering additional or supplemental services above and beyond what the client has requested, making the company a more attractive choice.

FUZZY LOGIC 2.3

"Loyal customers expect a good price, but they crave value most of all."

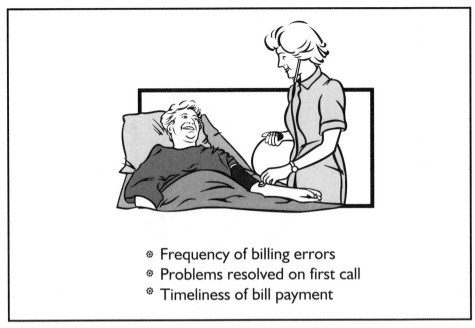

Figure 2–6.   Therefore, we need to measure . . .

Rather than becoming an enemy, price can be a tool to filter out buyers who'll bolt anyway for a penny. As shown in Figure 2–7, the challenge is to weigh price issues in balance with quality issues to maximize the customer perception of value. The customer relationship measurement techniques described in subsequent chapters will assist in accomplishing this balance.

FUZZY LOGIC 2.4

"The company with the most information wins!"

Therefore, in today's market, the ideal corporate management measurement system would include the internal financial data integrated with external market share information, and an ongoing report on customer satisfaction as shown in Figure 2–8. Because of the importance of the customer satisfaction index (described later), it seems only logical that in the customer-focused future, corporate annual reports will include a page on customer satisfaction as a forecast of the company's future success in the eyes of the current customers.

Homogeneous customers have gone from the marketplace, and been replaced by fragmented markets with varied needs. Diversity in customer demands will accelerate throughout the 1990s. The traditional great assimila-

Figure 2–7. The balance of customer-perceived value.

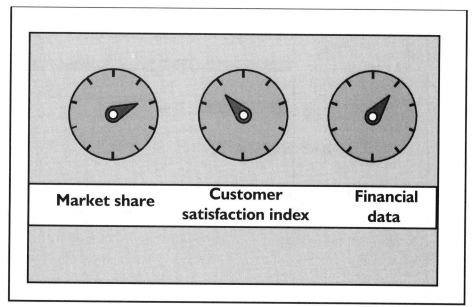

Figure 2–8. The complete company measurement system.

tor, the American middle class, is declining as a market force. The ranks of the affluent, the blue-collar, ethnic groups, and poor households will swell to make up the difference.

CUSTOMER SATISFACTION

What Is It?

A survey conducted by the accounting firm of Ernst and Young of 750 CEOs (Figure 2–9) shows that top management has awakened to the importance of satisfying the customer, and the importance of motivated employees (Ernst & Young, 1990). The majority of CEOs are trying to take steps to re-engineer critical processes to focus more on internal and external customer satisfaction.

Of Fortune 500 companies responding to a recent study conducted by Purdue University researchers, 87 percent specifically mention customer satisfaction in their corporate mission statement. Ironically, however, only 18 percent had in place a viable method of measuring this illusive metric, and none were compensated based on customer satisfaction (Anton, 1994).

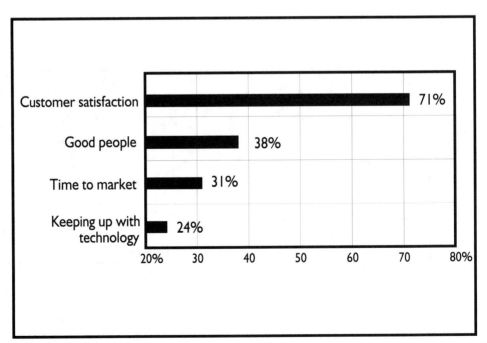

Figure 2–9. The biggest challenge for the next five years.

Customer satisfaction is the link between short-term success and long-term growth and prosperity. Corporations of all sizes are realizing that customer satisfaction

- Is a critical strategic weapon that results in increased market share and increased profits
- Begins with the commitment of top management
- Involves the entire organization
- Can be quantified, measured, and tracked
- Has fundamental organizational structure implications

FUZZY LOGIC 2.5

> *"Customer satisfaction is a state of mind in which his or her needs, wants, and expectations throughout the product/service life have been meet or exceeded, resulting in repurchase and loyalty."*

Figure 2–10 shows how the total quality management paradigm of the 1980s can be combined with the customer relationship focus of the 1990s to produce maximum customer satisfaction and brand loyalty. By creating

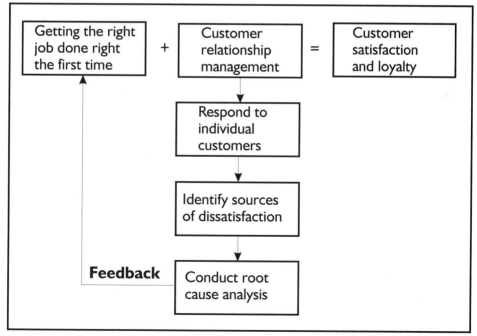

Figure 2–10. Maximizing cutomer satisfaction.

"feedback loops" of customer responses, the corporate enterprise becomes a learning system with the customer dictating the objectives and priorities.

FUZZY LOGIC 2.6

> *"Satisfied customers will (a) repurchase your products/services, (b) recommend your products/services to others, and (c) generate positive word of mouth."*

The critical success factors for a customer relationship strategy that delivers the value expected by today's customers are shown in Figure 2–11.

The Value of It

In comparing and contrasting unhappy customers with happy customers, the U.S. Office of Consumer Affairs (Knauer, 1992) produced the data summarized in Figure 2–12. Surveys of unhappy, or dissatisfied, customers become an important link in continuously improving customer relationships.

You might ask, "Why didn't these customers complain before switching

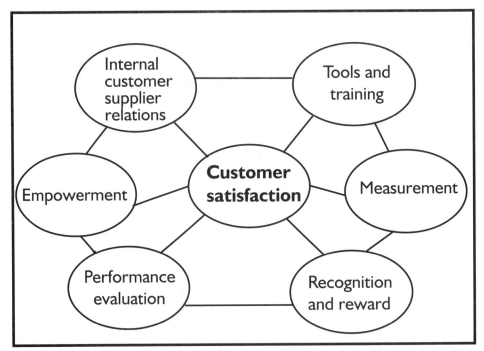

Figure 2–11.   Critical success factors.

Unhappy customers

Only 4 percent of dissatisfied customers complain.

Over 90 percent of unhappy customers won't be back.

Each dissatisfied customer tells nine other people.

Happy customers

Retaining customers costs one-fifth to one-sixth less.

Satisfied customers are willing to pay more.

Each happy customer will tell five people about good service.

Figure 2–12. The value of customer satisfaction.

to other products or services?" The answer is simple, "Our culture does not place much value on revealing negative feelings." Instead, we're taught "Keep a stiff upper lip," or "Don't be a whiner," or "Big boys don't cry." Voting with our feet is the American Way.

According to same study noted above, only 4 percent of dissatisfied customers ever give us feedback about their unhappiness. The other 96 percent vote with their feet, and 91 percent of unhappy customers will never come back again. Sadly, the study also found that most dissatisfied customers would have returned if there had been a professional attempt to save them at the time of the negative incident.

Our focus in this book is on developing a customer relationship measuring system to enhance the management process so we can tune in to every wish and need of individual customers. Customers often have valuable suggestions to improve a process, even though these suggestions frequently sound like complaints. Complaints are really just mistakes we've made in the eyes of individual customers.

FUZZY LOGIC 2.7

"The customer, of course, is always right."

A person only complains if he or she can conceive of something better, or has experienced something better. Therefore, we should always ask a complaining customer for his or her opinion of what would be a "better way." You'll be amazed what you find out—a gold mine of opportunities. Each complaint is a way to serve a particular customer differently, and as such, is an opportunity.

Research reveals that delivering high-quality service is closely linked to profits, cost savings, and market share in many industries. Studies have found that increased profits are due to several factors:

1. Fewer customer defections
2. Stronger customer loyalty
3. Long-lasting customer relationships
4. More cross-selling of products and services at higher margins

We have mentioned several times how important it is for loyal customers to say good things (positive word of mouth) about our company and its products/services. Figure 2–13 shows the results of a study conducted by General Electric's market researchers (Clemmer, 1993) indicating the over-

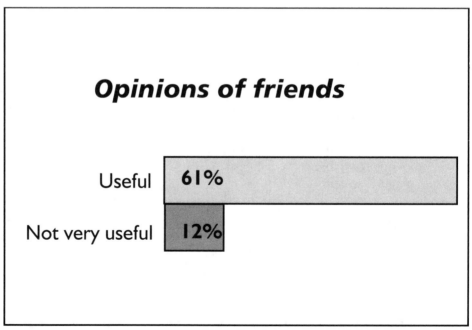

Figure 2–13. In prepurchase situations, word-of-mouth matters.

whelming importance consumers place on the opinions of friends before making a purchase decision.

FUZZY LOGIC 2.8

> *"Positive word of mouth will not necessarily get you the sale; however, negative word of mouth essentially guarantees you will not get the sale."*

Basic Approaches to Measuring It

Customer relationships can be measured qualitatively (explained in Chapter 3) and quantitatively (explained in Chapter 4). Although these very important techniques will be discussed in some depth later, suffice it to say for now that within these two categories there are two basic approaches to obtaining customer inputs:

1. *The planned approach.* The planned approach entails corporate initiatives to seek out both internal and external customer inputs on a proactive basis. This includes comment cards, surveys, focus groups, and others.
2. *The event-driven approach.* The event-driven approach entails being ready to accept customer inputs when the customer reaches out to the company. This might include having a toll-free number available when a customer is in trouble with your product, specifically monitoring and managing complaints, gathering information when there is a warranty claim, and the like.

The Customer Satisfaction Model

FUZZY LOGIC 2.9

> *"A moment of truth is defined as every opportunity that the customer has to experience and evaluate his or her relationship with your company."*

As Figure 2–14 shows, there are really only three possibilities: You deliver more than expected, as expected, or less than expected. The customer will subconsciously grade or score the relationship after each experience, no matter how subtle, and the accumulation of all these scores determines whether the customer will buy from you again in the future. Case 5 in Chapter 10 is an example of this effect.

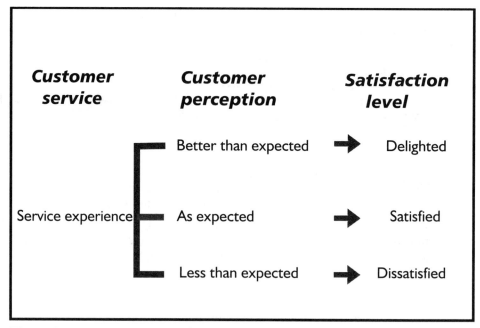

Figure 2–14.   Every moment-of-truth counts.

In Figure 2–15 we have divided customers into three distinct segments: those that are dissatisfied, those that are satisfied, and those that are delighted. Research has shown that customers will react very differently depending on which of the three states of mind they are in at the time (Anton & deRuyter, 1991). These differences show up in the following actions:

1. Willingness to recommend
2. Intentions to repurchase
3. Positive word of mouth

According to an often quoted study by the Xerox Corporation (Freedman, 1993):

FUZZY LOGIC 2.10

"A delighted customer is six times more likely to repurchase your product or service than a satisfied customer."

Customer loyalty and willingness to repurchase is not a linear relationship as is clearly shown in Figure 2–16 (Reichheld & Sasser, 1990). Delighted

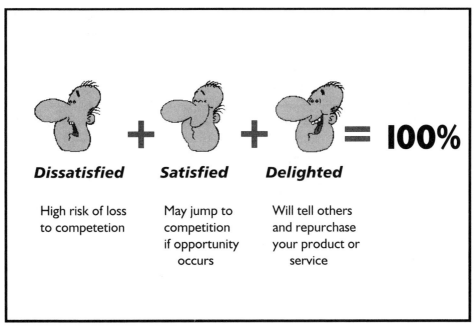

Figure 2–15. Typical customer segments.

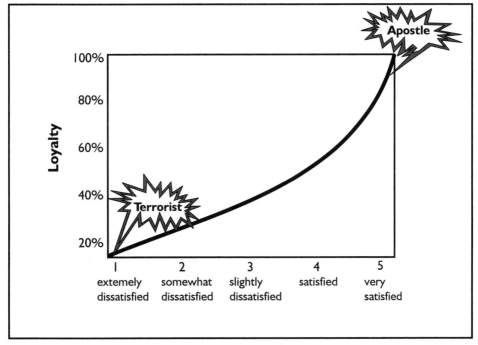

Figure 2–16. Why it pays to delight your customers.

customers can result literally in generations of repeat customers—for example, the John Deere Company likes to measure customer loyalty in terms of generations of farming families that have used its products.

Our challenge is take all the sources of customer feedback and combine these into simple to read and understand reports with which management can take clear action. The steps to accomplished this are summarized in Figure 2–17. Customer input emanates from many sources, or customer listening posts, and can be captured by the information technology system of choice for analysis and feedback. The challenge is to develop and implement an executive information system (EIS) that will keep top management finely tuned with the customer on a daily basis.

Ultimately, our goal is to develop a set of customer-focused metrics that can be used by management in concert with financially focused metrics to improve the quality of corporate planning and execution. Such a system would look like Figure 2–18.

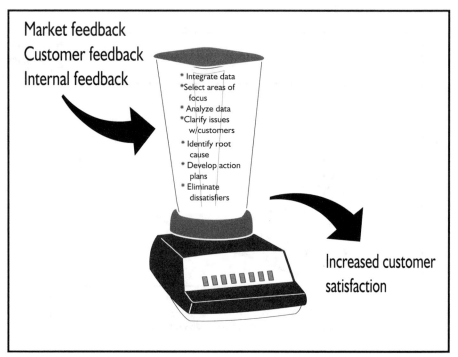

Figure 2–17.   Data from customer listening posts.

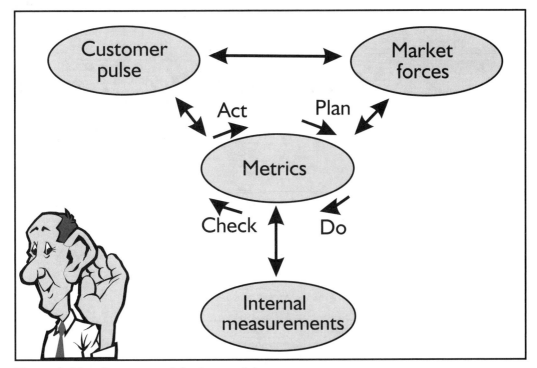

Figure 2–18. Customer satisfaction model.

LESSONS

LEARNED

✔ Measuring customer satisfaction is key to customer relationship management.

✔ Companies need to combine financial metrics with customer metrics for more effective long-range decision making.

✔ Today's customers focus on value, which is best described as quality divided by price.

✔ Unhappy customers are frequently an untapped source of ideas for change, and at the same time, if consulted, can be won over to become loyal clients.

✔ Inputs may be obtained from customers qualitatively and quantitavely.

3

Qualitative Measurement Methods

INTRODUCTION

This book is a testimony to the management revolution that the information era has brought forth by providing us the capability to track, report, and analyze customer relationship data quickly and efficiently. This information revolution really began quietly with binary coding, and exploded into the power of modern technology, handling extremely complex numerical calculations on coded customer data. The information revolution has been first and foremost a quantitative revolution.

While qualitative data were not ignored in the process, they have taken something of a back seat. In a real sense, qualitative aspects of research issues only got the full attention of the information juggernaut when they could be coded in a manner appropriate to quantitative treatment.

In particular, if a qualitative statement could be posed such that customers could respond to it on a Likert-type scale (for example, a 1 to 5 scale with 1 = completely disagree, 5 = completely agree), then the power of a PC-based statistics software package, such as SPSS (our choice for this book), could be brought to bear and the tracking, interpretation, and reporting functions could be carried out (Spector, n.d.).

An example Likert scale statement might be, "The ABC company gives prompt service." The scores on each such statement can then be aggregated and correlated to overall satisfaction to give a numeric rating of a company's customer service performance. This process will be explained in detail later.

Despite such efforts, qualitative measurement has been a poor brother to quantitative customer relationship measurement. In many cases, qualitative has been confined to one or two open-ended questions on a lengthy quantitative survey, with little effort expended on the interpretation of the answers. In such cases, the very interaction of wordy answers to quantitative analysis has relegated the information to secondary status.

Yet qualitative techniques have been developed in other fields of measurement, to a status almost equal to that of quantitative work. A case in point is marketing, where focus group techniques are today almost commonplace. Customer relationship management, with its accent on customers' attitudes and expectations, is an area particularly ripe for the application of qualitative techniques. In this chapter, we will outline the most popular of these techniques.

QUALITATIVE MEASUREMENT DEFINED

FUZZY LOGIC 3.1

> *"Qualitative measurement probes the environment surrounding an observed phenomenon."*

For example, suppose measurement of the above described survey had shown that a company had a low score on employees' courtesy. The next piece of information you need to know is, "What was it about the way my employees dealt with their customers that generated such a low score?" For this you might turn to face-to-face interviews with some of your best customers, where you can ask them what they think about the way they were treated by the employees.

In this example, the qualitative measurement came after the quantitative study, and was used to put some flesh on the bare bones of statistical numbers. Now suppose the phenomenon of interest was customers' attitudes to a change in the company's billing practices. Eventually, you will find out the customer's attitudes to the changes as people contact the company's call-center and post their complaints. You may also carry out a questionnaire survey of your customers and find out what they thought of the changes. But, let's say you need information now, to make sure you have not made any errors that could cause market damage (see Case 2 in Chapter 10 for a discussion on market damage).

What you could do is organize a panel meeting of regular customers to critically discuss the new billing practices. If there are aspects of the practices that the panel finds unacceptable, you could probe why the panel found the practices unacceptable, and ask them how you could make them more palatable.

We will see in Chapter 6 how qualitative data can be acquired in conjunction with quantitative data through the inclusion of open-ended questions in a survey. If we wish to know more about a response to, say, a yes/no question, we can follow it with a question such as, "If you answered NO to the previous question, please explain why."

The open-ended question is particularly effective on a comment card. A comment card usually asks a small number of Likert scale or yes/no questions about a consumer product or service. A final question inviting the respondent to express any other concerns gives customers the opportunity to explain their quantitative answers or to add to the information with qualitative data.

In what follows, we will concentrate on three qualitative techniques that are free-standing, in the sense that they can be carried out in their own right at any stage of customer relationship management. The techniques are (1) focus group interviews, (2) advisory panels, and (3) critical incident analysis.

FREE-STANDING QUALITATIVE TECHNIQUES

Focus Group Interviews

Focus group interviews are repeated interactive discussions among randomly selected customers of your product. The groups are fairly small, usually eight to twelve people, and each group contains different people. The group interaction is coordinated by a moderator, who uses an interview schedule or script to guide the discussion. The moderator will usually be a professional at the task who has worked with the sponsors of the research to develop the script.

The facilities dedicated to focus group research usually comprise an interview room with a table around which up to twelve people and a moderator can congregate, with one-way mirrors for the sponsors to observe the proceedings, and built in microphones and video cameras to record the sessions.

The operators of the facilities will arrange catering for attendees and will provide for transcripts of tapes, if required. Most operators will supply the moderator and even do the leg work required to guarantee that customers attend on the planned day. Fees for all of this are usually priced on a per group meeting basis, and can vary from about $2,500 to $7,500 or more, depending on the inputs required for the session. Our experience suggests that after the fourth session, the marginal yield of new information diminishes, so that four meetings will often be sufficient (Anton, Bennett, & Widdows, 1994).

Given that the procedural part of the measurement can be contracted out, the emphasis for the customer relationship manager needs to be placed on two aspects of the interviews: the content of the interview schedule (script) and the analysis of the data.

The script for the focus groups should be developed in conjunction with the moderator, since much will depend on the moderator's style. Some moderators prefer very directed scripts, wherein the questions are ordered in a sequential manner, and all possible contingencies are thought through. Room can be created at appropriate places in the script to follow likely diversions to a conclusion. Such scripts are lengthy and cumbersome. At the other extreme, there are moderators who prefer a looser script that covers only the bare bones of the topic plus some hints as to directions to follow. These types of scripts are shorter and somewhat cryptic. Figure 3–1 shows one such script, which was used in a focus group conducted by Purdue University researchers to study customers' attitudes about car rental services.

The choice of a directed versus an undirected interview schedule depends on the subject at issue as well as the moderator's preferred style. Where the specifics of customer service are under discussion, a directed approach may be better, to make sure that all aspects of current service offerings are reviewed. An undirected script is often useful when more general issues are being discussed, such as company image among customers, or customers' expectations for the future. More experienced moderators often prefer the undirected script, and will rely on feedback from the sponsors during the session to make sure that the questions sponsors wish to have answers to are fully covered.

Analysis of results of the focus group sessions can be left to the moderator, but there are advantages in doing one's own analysis. Primarily, as the sponsor, you would know the background to the issues being discussed and could therefore better identify the focus of the discussion. The major disadvantage of doing one's own analysis is that analysis of focus group data is a laborious process and requires the input of several people.

Analysis of the data involves the viewing of the tapes of the groups by a team of two or three people who will try to identify the common themes that emerged from the meetings. This will require notetaking, replaying, and discussion among the team. Once the common themes are identified, they must be articulated in report format, with illustrations from the content of individual meetings.

1. Introduction
   a. Go around the group and introduce each other.
   b. Explain how focus groups work.
2. Use of rental cars
   a. How frequently do respondents use rental cars?
   b. For what purpose?
   c. Who pays the bill?
   d. Which company/companies do they use?
3. Attitude toward car rental
   a. Describe a "good" rental car experience you have had. Probe: What did the rental car company do to make it "good"?
   b. Describe a "bad" rental car experience. Probe: What could the rental car company have done to make it better?
   c. In general, what do you expect from a rental car company in terms of customer service?
4. Attitude toward rental car companies
   a. Which company do you perceive to be the leader in the industry? Probe: Why?
   b. Which company do you think is a dog? Probe: Why?
   c. What factors would determine how you rank rental car companies?
5. (Show promotion video)
   a. What do you think of the company in this advertisement?
   b. How much would you expect to pay for the company services?
   c. If it cost ($x) would you use this company's services? Probe: Why or why not?
   d. What factors would increase the probability of your using the company's services?
6. Closeout
   a. What did you think was the purpose of this session?
   b. Is there anything you would like to add to what you said here today?

Figure 3–1. Interview script for a focus group meeting on car rental experiences.

Inevitably, there will be idiosyncratic elements of each group's interactions. These are often the surprises of focus group research—items that often would not have occurred to anyone beforehand. These, too, need to be reported, either as special findings of each group, or as an itemized account of anomalies of the results.

When interpreting results, the researchers need to be cognizant of the dynamics of the groups. Was a point really agreed upon by a group, or was the group log-rolled by one dominant individual? Did a person tell the group what he or she really felt, or did the body language suggest otherwise? These issues must be resolved by the research team to the satisfaction of all members before conclusions are drafted in the final report.

A feature of reports of focus group meetings is the lack of tabulations and numerical interpretations of data. Occasional summary tables may be produced outlining, say, the number of times a particular issue was mentioned by a group, or the outcome of a vote in the group on a particular point (for example, how many of the group agreed that an issue applied to them). For the most part, however, the report relies on the narrative flow to get the points across. Case 4 in Chapter 10 has some similarities to the focus group approach just discussed. Focus group information should be limited to the qualitative insights of customer needs, and must in most cases be further investigated through quantitative methods described in later chapters.

Advisory Panels

Advisory panels, sometimes called CAPs (for customer advisory panels), are also repeated meetings of small groups of customers. The subject matter for the meetings is a company's relationship with its customers, and the meetings are guided by an agenda of items covering the customer service strategy. Panels are useful wherever business involves moments of truth with customers.

CAPs are particularly useful in a retail setting, where the agenda can cover any aspect of store policy, such as merchandise mix, store layout, store atmosphere, or employee conduct. Utility companies have had success with panels, with the agenda covering such diverse issues as safety, billing format, and policy toward handicapped and elderly consumers.

CAP members are usually deliberately chosen to represent larger subgroups of customers. There may, for example, be a member of an ethnic subgroup such as Hispanic customers, or of a particular socioeconomic subgroup such as the elderly. Depending on the agenda of the panel, there may be representatives of other kinds of interests, such as an environmentalist or someone from the local Chamber of Commerce. The general customer might be represented by one or two members drawn at large from the customer base.

It is the norm for CAPs to include company employees as members. In a retail panel, for example, store managers may be present to hear and respond to discussion of store policy. If possible, the upper level of management should be present, so that the concerns of customers can be appreciated at the top. In addition, the presence of upper management would send a signal that the customer is taken seriously within the organization. The number of company representatives to the panel should be kept low to prevent the panel from being overwhelmed.

Unlike the focus group, where a group meets once and is disbanded, CAP membership is long term, to develop continuity of action within the panel. A typical tenure of a member would be two years, with members rotated off sequentially so as not to disrupt the continuity of experience.

The main information component of a CAP is the minutes of the meetings. The minutes will contain any policy resolutions or recommendations made by the panel. It is then up to the company to act upon these recommendations and report the actions and their results back to the panel. The information so generated can be summarized in an annual report of the CAP's activities.

It is important to note that a CAP is a medium through which customers' attitudes and opinions about a company's customer relationships are transmitted to the company. It is not a means by which a company educates its customers about its policies. CAPs are a very inefficient customer education mechanism.

The success of a CAP depends upon the willingness and ability of company personnel to listen to and act upon its recommendations. If there is a legitimate, strong reason why a panel recommendation must be ignored, then the reason should be explained to the panel. To ignore panel recommendations will lead to disillusionment and low morale among panel members, and ultimately the demise of the CAP. If there are items of policy that the company knows in advance are not subject to change by the panel's suggestion, then these items should be excluded from the agenda up front, and the reasons explained to the panel, to prevent future misunderstandings.

The CAP annual report should be a celebration of its achievements, trumpeted to all levels of the company. The annual report is thus not a research document in the sense discussed elsewhere in this book. Nor is the panel a research instrument in the sense used here. The panel should be a partner in customer relationship management for the business. To be anything less is to waste a lot of people's time. Case 5 in Chapter 10 incorporates some elements of the advisory panel technique.

The Critical Incident Technique

The question of the interactions (moments of truth) between a company and its customers emerged as potential items for both a focus group script and a CAP agenda. When it comes to assessment of the quality of moments of truth and their potential importance to customer relationship management, a special technique from psychological research known as critical incident technique (CIT) can be brought to bear (Feinberg & Widdows, n.d.).

CIT uses detailed narratives to uncover the essence of moments of truth. What makes a moment of truth a good or bad experience for customers? What impression does the customer take away following a moment of truth? From the answers to these questions can come policy to improve the company's interactions with customers so that they contribute to the bottom line rather than cause market damage.

The underlying notion of CIT is that moments of truth contain the potential to develop into critical business situations. A bad moment of truth can generate anger among customers and lead to dissatisfaction, disputes, and lost business. A good moment of truth can lead to delight, loyalty, and good word of mouth.

Some moments of truth are more critical than others in this regard—for example, the cancellation of an airline flight or a billing error. And depending how the situations are handled by customer services representatives, the incidents can become ones of dispute or delight. Hence the importance of understanding the qualitative nature of the interaction.

CIT proceeds by asking customers to identify significant moments of truth and to relate their experiences. The information is generated by an open-ended question of a general form such as the following, which is from a mail questionnaire addressed to retail store customers:

> Think about a time when you had an outstandingly bad or good experience at our store. In the space below, describe the incident in detail, as it happened. In addition, please tell us what made it bad or good.

The question would be followed by one or two blank sheets for the respondent to fill in the narrative. Additional questions could be appended, covering items such as a customer satisfaction index or sociodemographic data about the respondent.

Since the objective of the CIT is to obtain a representative sample of the customer base, a large number of surveys would be required. The survey could be conducted by mail, by telephone, or even by face-to-face interviews. The former of these is most economical in terms of resources. With internal persons handling the data, a CIT study with a mail-out of about 1,000 questionnaires could be done for a budget of around $10,000. With external help, the budget could be up to ten times this amount or more, depending on the size of the sample and the technique for distributing the survey.

The major information component of the CIT is the narratives. The task facing researchers is to extract the content from the narratives, so that light can be shed on the moment of truth. This will involve a team of people sifting through each story, highlighting the key words and phrases that characterize the incident and its aftermath, and then compiling a report that summarizes the common themes and their variations.

Figure 3–2 contains the compilation of results of a CIT of university student experiences with banks, which was conducted by Purdue University in the fall of 1994. This study was experimental, in that instead of asking students for their actual consumer experiences, the researchers inquired about the ideal experience students would like to have. The idea was to explore customer marketing opportunities for banks that wished to delight their student customers. The research question was:

> We are carrying out a study of banking services from the standpoint of consumers' experience and would like your input. Think about and describe the ideal service you would like to receive from a bank, credit union, or similar financial institution.

Figure 3–2 is a quantitative presentation of a qualitative study. It reports not only what characterized the ideal incident, but how frequently the particular characteristics cropped up in a random sample of students. This unique quantitative—qualitative combination makes CIT a powerful technique for the evaluation of consumer affairs policy. Case 1 in Chapter 11 is an example of CIT.

Tips on What to Use When

Perhaps the biggest drawback to qualitative research is that (with the possible exception of CIT) the information comes from a small sample of people who cannot be regarded as being representative statistically of the broader population of customers.

Fuzzy Logic 3.2

> *"It is not only unwise, but potentially dangerous, to make major changes in customer relationship management policy based solely on a qualitative study."*

The problem here is the cost in terms of time and financial resources of obtaining a large enough random sample of qualitative opinion to make generalizations, and then of sifting through and summarizing the mountain of data that would be generated. CIT is a possible exception because it can be conducted in a questionnaire format, and the content analysis techniques can

1. The items mentioned in narratives about the ideal service fell into five categories, as follows:
    a. Services offered (147 mentions)
    b. Friendliness of personnel (83 mentions)
    c. Efficiency of personnel (83 mentions)
    d. Knowledgeability of employees (43 mentions)
    e. Office environment (17 mentions)
2. The principal services that comprise the ideal experience are as follows:
    a. Cost-free ATMs (23 mentions)
    b. Extended banking hours (18 mentions)
    c. Free checking (11 mentions)
    d. Higher interest rates (10 mentions)
    e. No service charges (8 mentions)
    f. No minimum balance (8 mentions)
    g. Lower rates on credit cards (7 mentions)
    h. Nationwide banking (6 mentions)
    i. Accurate banking statements (5 mentions)
    j. More ATMs (4 mentions).
3. Some typical responses were:

"The ideal banking service would be a bank that is open 24 hours a day."

"I would like a bank with no service fee for using ATM cards at machines other than their own."

"Free checking and low interest rates on credit cards."

Figure 3–2. Students' assessment of the ideal banking experience using a critical incident approach.

be applied fairly efficiently once the major themes of the narratives have been identified. Even so, when representative opinions of consumers are required, a quantitative survey is usually preferred.

This does not mean that qualitative measurement should be abandoned. Rather, it needs to be combined with a quantitative study so that the two complement each other. Indeed, it could be argued that a quantitative study undertaken without some attempt to probe the qualitative aspects will be insufficient to get across the subtleties and complexities of customer relationship management.

As a case in point, Purdue University researchers recently conducted a seminar session at a conference of marketing researchers in which they gave one-half the audience the results of a CIT and the other the results of a SERVQUAL index of customer attitudes to repair service for an electronic appliance (Berry, 1988). The audience was invited to offer three or four recommendations for changes in the repair service practices based on results. Although the two parts of the questionnaire were filled in by the same customers, the recommendations from the audience were different and to some degree contradictory. Once the results were combined, however, the policy recommendations became more direct and consistent.

This case study brings this chapter back to its starting point. Qualitative research is essential to a full understanding of customer relationship management issues. It puts the flesh on the bones of quantitative research. It can also enable the quantitative research to ask the right questions. For example, focus groups should be conducted to get an idea of product/service attributes that the customer thinks are important before a survey is drafted, as we will demonstrate in Chapter 6. The quantitative survey would then probe the performance and importance of the attributes to a statistical sample representative of all customers through a Likert-type scale.

In the case of CIT, a big enough survey can combine qualitative and quantitative aspects of moments of truth in one study, and open-ended questions can do the same for a questionnaire survey, provided enough people take the trouble to answer them. Finally, the reports of an advisory panel provide a running commentary on the way customers regard actual customer service offerings, and enable the company to fine tune its policies in real time. The whole package described above is a powerful one for those companies who truly wish to understand their customers and better manage this critical relationship.

LESSONS LEARNED

✔ Quantitative customer relationship measurement cannot be properly performed without proper qualitative research being conducted first.

✔ The best customer relationship measurement results are a combination of qualitative and quantitative.

✔ Perhaps the biggest drawback to qualitative research is that the information comes from a small sample of people who cannot be regarded as being representative statistically of the broader population of customers.

✔ Qualitative measurements put the flesh on the bones of quantitative research. They can also enable the quantitative research to ask the right questions.

✔ Three forms of qualitative measurements that we find useful are focus groups, advisory panels, and the critical incident technique.

4

Quantitative Measurement Methods

INTRODUCTION

The goal of this chapter is to begin the process of quantifying the link between the "voice of the customer " and internal process measures, also called internal metrics. We will first deal with how this quantification is done, in overview, leaving some of the real details for later chapters.

FUZZY LOGIC 4.1

"You cannot improve externally what you don't measure internally."

The reason so many companies fail to ultimately use data gathered from customer comment cards, surveys, and the like is that there is no direct connection between the outside measures and what to change internally. Our focus in this chapter will be to discover that linkage.

The concept of connecting internal metrics to external customer-perceived value is shown in Figure 4–1. The chapter presents the overview of the process with more details of measurement techniques found in Chapters 5, 6, and 7.

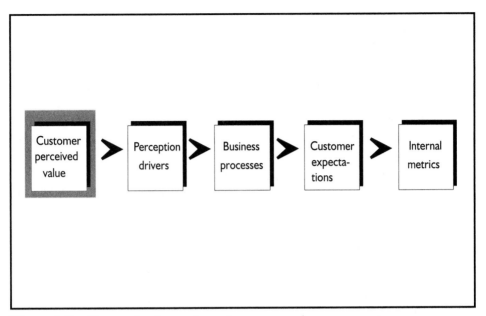

Figure 4–1. Connecting internal metrics to external measurements.

CONNECTING INTERNAL AND EXTERNAL METRICS

Let's begin with a brief discussion of what we mean by an internal metric that is "behaviorally anchored." First of all, an internal metric is an easily measured activity inside the company—for example, the time in hours, or days, it takes to issue a price quotation to a customer, or the frequency of mistakes in invoices. A behaviorally anchored metric is one where we can alter the numerical value of the metric by a change in employee behavior. In the examples above, that might mean issuing the price quotation in half the normal time by changing employee priorities, adding software or an additional printer. In the case of the invoices, a second employee could check the invoices to improve accuracy before they are sent to customers. To repeat, a behaviorally anchored metric is one where a change in employee behavior will either increase or decrease the numeric value of the metric.

FUZZY LOGIC 4.2

"Where possible, you should ensure that the internal metrics that you select are behaviorally anchored."

The second factor in selecting an internal metric is to ensure that changes in the metric, in fact, impact customer satisfaction, and this impact can be measured. Once established, internal metrics can be an effective method way to monitor customer satisfaction on a daily basis.

In the electronics industry, internal metrics might include: (1) average response time for a service call, (2) the total number of customers serviced in a day, and (3) the amount of time field service engineers spend searching for a telephone after they are paged. In the insurance industry, an internal metric might be: How long does it take to issue a policy after an application has been received by the home office?

In a call center, the level of service can be monitored by the average speed of answer (ASA) metric, or the average handle time (AHT) metric. It is important to emphasize, however, that the ideal internal metrics to monitor must be perceptible to the external customer.

At Federal Express the goal is "zero defects" leading to 100 percent customer satisfaction (Davidow & Uttal, 1989). Internal metrics that are closely monitored at 24-hour intervals include late deliveries and lost packages. Failures then are weighted for their importance to customers, providing the direct tie of internal measurement to customer-perceived value measurements.

Now that we have established what specific kinds of internal metrics we wish to monitor, let's begin with customer-perceived value and work our way back to internal metrics. As you saw from Figure 4–1, we must work our way from the customer to the customer perception drivers, to the business processes that touch the customer and produce the perception, to the customer's expectations of the business processes, and ultimately to the internal metric(s) that monitors the process.

MAPPING QUALITY PERCEPTION DRIVERS

FUZZY LOGIC 4.3

"Today's busy and cost-conscious customers focus almost exclusively on value."

Sayings like "Where can I get the best value for my money?" or "That automobile is your best overall value!" are heard all the time. Value, however is a very elusive measure that is a highly subjective judgment on the part of customers. We and others (Cronin & Taylor, 1992) have discovered value to be quality divided by price as shown in Figure 4–2. "The customer can rate

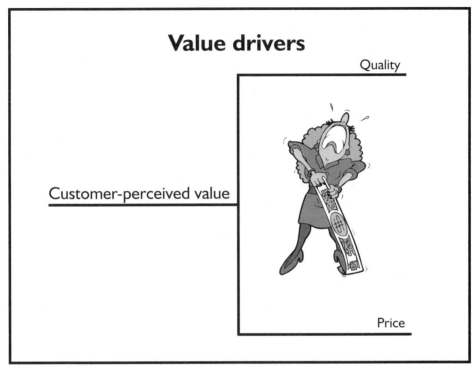

Value drivers

Quality

Customer-perceived value

Price

Figure 4–2. The customer wants "the most for the least."

us better or worse than somebody else. It's not very scientific, but it's disastrous if you score low!" (Mather, 1993).

FUZZY LOGIC 4.4

"Customers switch suppliers because they are not satisfied with the company's perceived value, relative to the competition."

Conformance to company specifications does not necessarily produce value as perceived by the customer. Conformance to customer needs and expectations leads directly to customer-perceived value.

Many companies have a natural "knee-jerk" for increasing value, and that is to cut price, that is, the ratio of quality to price increases with a decrease in price. This can work as a very short-term strategy, however, it is sadly short-sighted for the long term. Unfortunately, when working with the price part of value, you have really only two choices—reduce cost and/or reduce margins. Neither alternative is that attractive in today's competitive markets; after all, you can only cut costs so far before cutting "to the bone," and who wants to keep giving up margins!

Let's go on to Figure 4–3 and briefly define each of the quality perception drivers (Rust, Zahorik, & Keiningham, 1994).

1. *The product usability driver* is the customer's overall impression of tangible experiences as part of a business relationship. In its simplest form, it is the car you buy at a dealership or the meal you eat at a restaurant. In its more subtle form, it is the monthly bank statement you get from a bank or the policy you get from an insurance company. Product usability is the capacity of a product or service to satisfy the essence of a customer's need, want, or expectation. For example, the automobile to most customers is really "flexible transportation," the railroad train is really "mass transportation," and the certificate of deposit is "a safe spot to put my money with a guaranteed return."

2. *The service strategy driver* is all those plans and policies you make in anticipation of the customer's arriving to purchase your product or

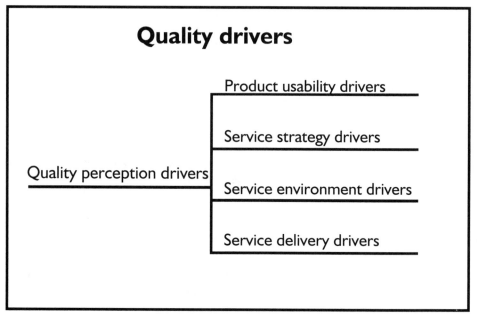

Figure 4–3.   The critical success factors of quality.

service. In the retail business, this would include the store hours, and return policies; in the consumer electronics business, this would include the product pricing, credit offerings, as well as the standard warranty period. For example, a major copier manufacturer recently added a three-year, everything-included guarantee. This fits the number one problem with copy machines, namely breakdowns.

3. *The service environment driver* is composed of all physical surroundings that facilitate the delivery of your product or service. This driver encompasses three distinct elements, namely:
    a. The ambient conditions—lighting, background music, temperature
    b. The spatial layout—entrances, lobbies, restrooms, counters, seating arrangements
    c. The signs and symbols—posters, flags, pennants, and the like.
    A rather simple example of this driver might by the importance that customers of luxury automobiles place on the sound of closing the door as an indication of quality. No matter how much high-tech engineering goes under the hood, or how much comfort goes into the seats, if the doors sound tinny, quality perception is negatively affected.

    Another example would be the exciting sound of the Harley Davidson engine when heard through its muffler. Aficionados will say, "I can hear it's a Harley from a mile away!" That's customer-perceived quality.

4. *The service delivery driver* is everything that actually happens when the service strategy is carried out by the employees. This includes primarily the customer's perception of employee attributes such as reliability, responsiveness, product knowledge, accuracy, empathy, and the like.

Most CEOs, when they are confronted with how to improve customer relationships, focus on the "people" part, or the service delivery driver. Figure 4–3 enables better understanding of the fact that the customer's perception of quality comes from these four very different driver categories, any one of which can diminish customer-perceived value. For example, how would you perceive the value of an airline ticket where the flight attendants treated you fantastically well, but served overdone steak with underdone potatoes, and the flight arrived 30 minutes late?

FUZZY LOGIC 4.5

> *"The proper goal is to achieve superior customer relationship value in areas that matter to the customer, together with a cost structure no higher than that of lower quality competitors."*

Astute companies communicate their products' unique customer-valued advantages through advertising and other marketing communications. When the customer perceives the quality and the exceptional value offered, a power brand is born. Dominant market share follows. There is really no magic here. Customer relationship drivers can be studied quantitatively through properly implemented information technology. Customer-driven ideas will be instantly visible through actionable reports coming from the customer information system.

Frank Perdue, of Perdue Chicken fame, succeeded because he listened to how the customer perceived and defined value in a chicken. According to marketing legend (Zeithaml, Parasuraman, & Berry, 1990), Frank bought a turbine engine to blow-dry his chickens to better eliminate pinfeathers. He was making a capital investment that neither expanded capacity nor cut costs. He was simply responding to what his surveys told him was a customer-perceived value driver, that is, featherless chickens. Customers perceived greater value in buying chickens with no feathers, and Frank gave it to them. His now-famous TV spots then focused on this product usability attribute as demanded by the consumer. Frank taught us that not only is listening important, but educating the consumer using what you have learned by listening is crucial to marketing success.

Having described the drivers of customer-perceived quality, we still do not have anything specific to measure and monitor for management purposes. Therefore, we will next explore the business processes that make up each of the quality drivers shown in Figure 4–3.

MOVING BEYOND PERCEPTION TO INTERNAL METRICS

If we take any one of the quality perception drivers—for example, the service strategy driver—we need to better understand what business processes comprise this driver. As shown in Figure 4–4, the service strategy of most compa-

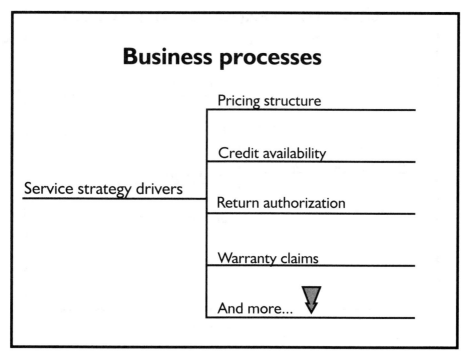

Figure 4–4. Business processes that comprise service strategy.

nies would include such planned strategy-related items as pricing, credit, returns, and warranty, to name only a few.

Next we must determine the customer's expectations when using each of these processes. We will discuss in Chapter 6 how to determine these expectations, but for now let's explore the warranty claims process, as shown in Figure 4–5. We might anticipate customer expectations to include such process attributes as simple paperwork, no hassles, rapid payment of claim, fairness in negotiations, and so on.

The last step is to connect each customer expectation to one or more behaviorally anchored internal metrics. Figure 4–6 shows several examples of internal metrics that could be used to monitor and improve the customer's expectation of simple paperwork for warranty claims; namely, the number of inquiries on how to fill out the claims form, number of submitted forms that must be resubmitted, and number of complaints about the amount of paperwork required for one claim.

Figure 4–7 illustrates the complete sequence from the external customer's perception to the internal metric that is anchored to employee behavior. In the next section we will present an overview on how and what to measure.

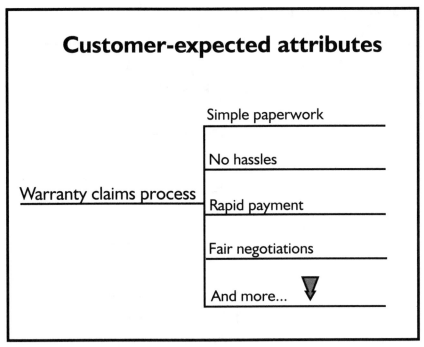

Figure 4–5. Business process attributes and customer expectations.

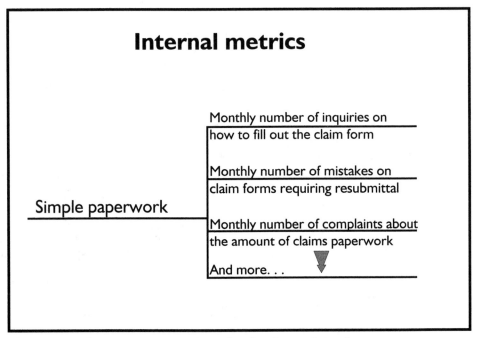

Figure 4–6. A customer expectation related to internal metrics.

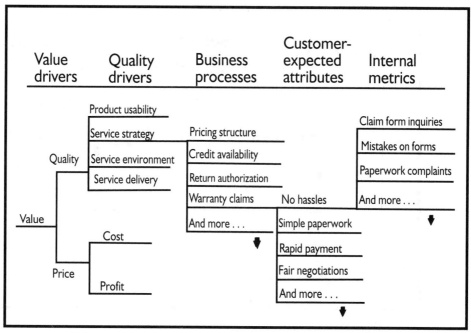

Figure 4–7. Making the quantitative connection.

SEARCHING FOR SOMETHING TANGIBLE
TO MEASURE

Customers consistently expect very specific attributes in virtually all products and services. Their top priorities include ease of use, timeliness, certainty, consistency, accuracy, and more. Companies, unfortunately, very rarely measure their performance in delivering on these attributes as judged by the customer. Lack of any consist form of measurement makes it virtually impossible to progressively address customer expectations and make improvements.

Looking back briefly at Figure 4–7, we will be describing the basic techniques for measuring the company's ability to deliver at or above customer expectations and ultimately relating this performance to an internal metric. Figure 4–8 depicts the concept of the measurement process commonly called gap analysis, which we will use throughout the remainder of this book (Shetty, 1993). The actual quantification of the gap is covered in detail in Chapter 6, however, suffice it to say for now that we can calculate a performance index, on a scale of from 0 to 100, on each customer perception of each company process.

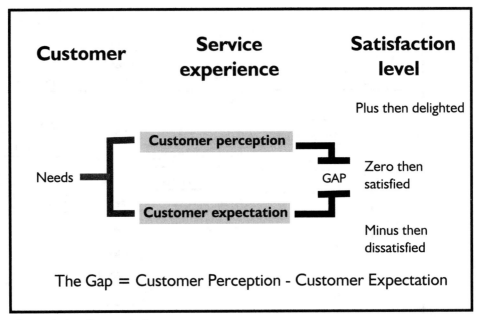

Figure 4–8. Gap analysis.

During the same period of time that we take the measure of the company's performance on each customer expectation, we also measure the value of the "connected" internal metric. For example, in Figure 4–6, as we measure our performance on "simple paperwork" for a warranty claim, we also note the average numerical value of the internal metrics listed. This is what gives us an insight into what to manage and change internally to improve the customer perception of our warranty claims paperwork. Without constant feedback from customers, a company can produce a defect-free buggy whip that no one wants.

DEVELOPING THE IMPACT FACTOR OF PERFORMANCE

Sometimes companies address and fix problems based solely upon the attribute in a survey that scores the lowest. Unfortunately, the "squeaky wheel gets the oil." In many situations, however, the attribute that has the lowest score may not be the attribute that is the most important driver of customer-perceived value and satisfaction.

The same is true of customer complaints. There is not a one-to-one relationship between complaint frequency and need for immediate change. Beware that the vocal minority doesn't cause your company to address the "gripes, swipes, and snipes" of a minority of customers while missing the real deal-breaker problems being experienced by the silent majority of customers.

Let's take the example shown in Figure 4–9, which shows the performance of the customer service representatives (CSRs) in delivering on the expectations of callers (how to calculate performance is described in Chapter 6). Notice that the lowest performing attribute is "was flexible," which means obviously that the callers on average felt that the company's CSRs working in the call center were not as flexible as expected. The call center manager might conclude that he or she should train the CSRs to be more flexible— "Give the customers what they want, and be more flexible" might be the instruction.

Before concluding that the CSRs should work on "flexibility," we recommend that you use multiple regression analysis to correlate each attribute to the caller's overall satisfaction with his or her call. Regression analysis is used to identify which attributes can be considered to be most influential in determining caller satisfaction. This very common statistical process can be simpli-

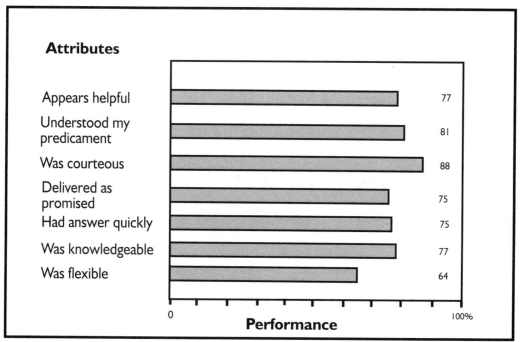

Figure 4–9. Attribute performance comparison.

fied and visualized by placing survey responses on an X-Y plot as shown in Figure 4–10. We have plotted the customers' survey responses to "Overall, how satisfied were you with the call to our center?" against the response to the statement "The CSR was flexible." Notice the points are quite scattered and seem unrelated.

By contrast, in Figure 4–11, we have plotted the customers' survey responses to "Overall, how satisfied were you with the call to our center?" against the response to the statement "The CSR appears helpful." Notice, by contrast, the points are not as scattered and the dotted line through the points is at an angle. This somewhat simplified statistical interpretation is that the attribute "appears helpful" is much more important to the customer, that is, has greater impact on the caller's satisfaction than "was flexible." In this example, we have assumed a simple linear environment displayed with one independent variable (helpful) and one dependent variable (overall satisfaction). Multiple regression accounts for all independent variables in the customer environment simultaneously by holding all others constant while looking at each one separately.

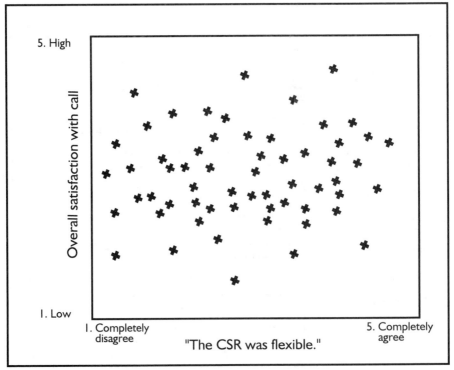

Figure 4–10. Attribute impact diagram.

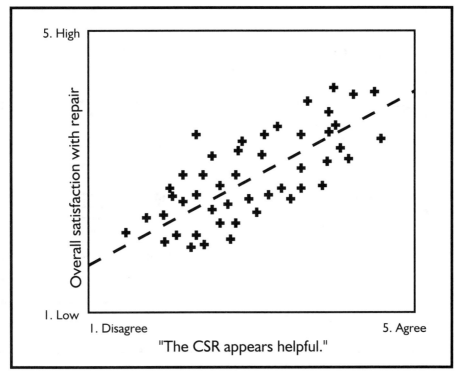

Figure 4–11. Attribute impact diagram.

In Figure 4–12, we have regraphed the CSR attributes to show both the call center's performance on each attribute as well as the customer impact on each attribute. Notice that this more in-depth output gives us greater insight into the voice of the customer and, in fact, might cause the center's manager to focus his or her CSRs on appearing more helpful as a way of increasing caller satisfaction.

This is a simple example of "getting it right per the customers' expectations." Customer expectation measurement is a many-faceted science. Often companies try to simplify the process by doing an occasional (typically once a year) "do you still love us" survey. Because of the way the survey is designed, the results are often high scores that make the company's CEO feel good but, in fact, are pure garbage and seldom uncover opportunities for improvement.

The fact is that a company that is serious about customer relationship management must commit to a continual measurement process, much like the logic behind having an accounting system with continuous financial controls in place. Only a very irresponsible company would measure financial data once a year.

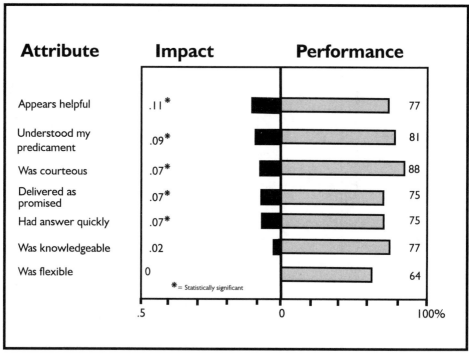

Figure 4–12.   Attribute performance and impact.

USING A STRATEGIC IMPROVEMENT MATRIX

The old saying, "It's not what you say, but how you say it," is in a small way also applicable to the presentation of customer data.

FUZZY LOGIC 4.6

"The better soft data is presented to management, the greater the likelihood action will be taken."

In our goal of facilitating "making hard decisions with soft numbers," how the soft results are presented can often be key to management's adoption of the results. A common complaint of customer relationship professionals is, "I present my management with all kinds of great reports, but no action is ever taken!"

One additional tool we recommend you have in your measurement toolbox, then, is what is called the strategic decision matrix, as shown in Figure

4–13. Each attribute from Figure 4–12 can roughly be placed in one of the quadrants for decision-making purposes. For example, "CSR was flexible" would be in the lower left corner and therefore not targeted for improvement. The problem with Figure 4–13 is how to decide what is high/low performance and/or low/high impact. Where are the boundary lines? How do you decide the ones that are not obvious? For example, again taking an attribute from Figure 4–12, where would you place "CSR was courteous"?

In order to give some definition of the boundary conditions, we developed the decision matrix in Figure 4–14 specifically for customer performance/impact data. Here is how it works. The vertical axis, or Impact, is divided into Yes or No, with the dividing line being simply whether the attribute's performance is having a significant impact on overall customer satisfaction. For example, from Figure 4–12, "CSR understood my predicament" would be above the line, or in the Yes zone.

The horizontal axis is divided at 85 percent (4.45 on the typical 5-point Likert scale). The reason for selecting 4.45 comes from the study (Freedman, 1993) depicted in Figure 2-16. The study shows that loyalty or willingness to repurchase is almost six times greater when respondents select a score of 5

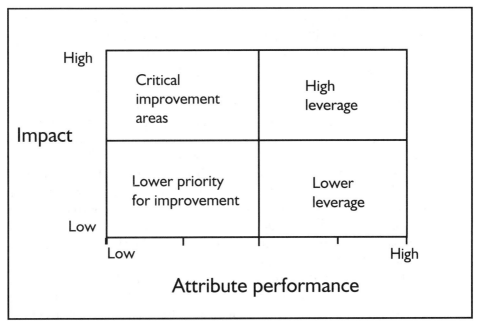

Figure 4–13. Strategic improvement matrix.

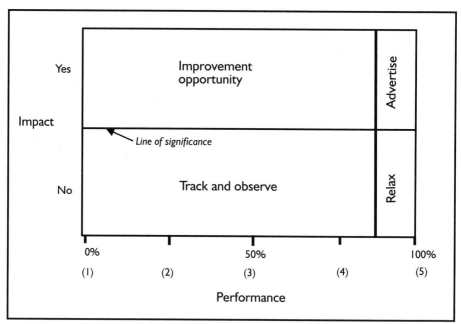

Figure 4–14. Decision matrix.

in rating company performance. Therefore, we rationalized that the top box, that is, the top right box, is an area where the customer is delighted with the performance on a statistically important attribute. We suggest that such product/service attributes should be part of the company's advertising message.

By contrast, the upper left box is for those attributes that statistically impact satisfaction, but where the company is scoring low in performance. We suggest that attributes in this box could be targeted for continuous improvement initiatives or ful-scale re-engineering.

As an example, we have taken all the attributes from Figure 4–12 and placed them in the appropriate boxes of the decision matrix shown in Figure 4–15. As you can see, only one attribute, "CSR was courteous," lands in the top box. The matrix would suggest that the CSRs focus on "keeping their promises," and that information technology should be investigated to help CSRs get "answers more quickly."

Lastly, by quantitative benchmarking of your closest competitor, the decision matrix in Figure 4–15 can become even more powerful. Imagine placing your competitor's performance scores for the same attributes on the same decision matrix. Your course of action becomes even more clear.

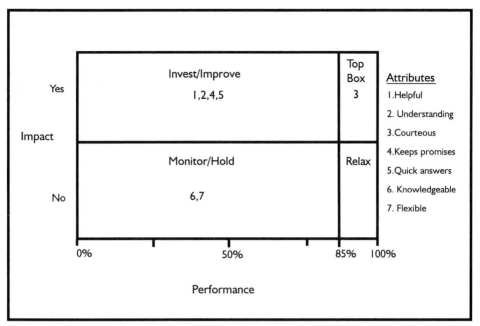

Figure 4–15. Decision matrix example.

LESSONS LEARNED

✔ The customer relationship measurement system must connect or link internal metrics to external customer evaluations.

✔ Internal metrics are most effective if behaviorally anchored.

✔ Gap analysis allows us to measure the statistical difference between customer expectations and their perceptions.

✔ Low performance on a process attribute does not necessarily target it for improvement.

✔ By statistically calculating "impact," we can better understand which attribute is important for our focus change.

5

Calculating Relationship Indices

INTRODUCTION

The main reason customer relationship data is not commonly used in business management stems from the lack of an organized and logical methodology in which customer data can be presented and interpreted for decision making.

The problem is not that the customer data isn't being collected. In fact, in most companies, there are numerous individuals doing surveys, conducting focus groups, monitoring critical incidents, and organizing advisory panels. Unfortunately, there is seldom a coordinated effort in these initiatives to gather data uniformly, process it consistently, present it logically, and interpret it for management. In many cases, these individuals would receive an A-plus for effort and intentions, but an F-minus for results in initiating corporate changes on behalf of the customer. There is seldom one holistic picture of the customer relationship situation that develops from a highly fragmented approach.

Contrast this to the painstakingly accurate and organized methodology of financial accounting. There are rules and regulations, even national Generally Adopted Accounting Procedures (GAAP). Financial accounting professionals begin with a university degree followed frequently by certification, that is, certified public account (CPA). In companies there are whole departments of accounting professionals and their staffs (lovingly called "bean counters") whose sole purpose is to keep track of the company's financial numbers.

Frequently, the "hard" numbers of financial accounting—dollars and cents—are compared (sometimes jokingly) to the "soft" numbers of customer relationship measurement. In this book, we accept the fact that customer numbers are going to be soft by the mere fact that they measure the less-than-precise attitudes and opinions of people. Nevertheless, we are convinced that by applying the methods described in this book, companies can learn how to "make hard decisions with soft numbers" about customer expectations and perceptions, and that making proactive decisions that are what the customer actually wants will do more to drive the company to financial success than endless reviews of the "hard" financial numbers of past performance.

Naturally, when those in charge of customer relationship management try to compete for top-executive time with those in charge of preparing and presenting the financial numbers, there is simply no contest. The army of accountants fortified with a major corporate budget can easily overwhelm the lesser endowed, and certainly less organized customer relationship managers. Therefore, frequently, the voice of the customer is not heard over the din of financial reporting and concerns.

We can learn a great deal from how the financial professionals deal with top management. We would summarize a few of these as follows:

1. Their methods of financial data capture are consistent and methodical.
2. Their use of information technology is extensive.
3. Their reports are timely and accurate.
4. They provide ratios, indices, and interpretation along with their reports.
5. Their reports are frequently in graphical form for ease of trend identification.
6. They compare this year's performance with last year (or years) to show important changes.

The incredible, but noteworthy, fact that does impress their executive audience (and should guide our reporting design) is that they can take reams of financial data and reduce it to two reports, typically listed on three pages. These reports are commonly known as the Balance Sheet and the Income Statement and are literally the most widely read reports of any company.

In our work with corporate executives, we have been asked over and over again, "Is there some way to reduce all of the customer relationship measurements to one or two numbers that I can use to guide my company?" We have developed such a system of computed indexes that can guide top management in a way similar to the financial reports. As we discussed in Chapter

2, Figure 2–8, the best combination of inputs to manage a company are financial, market share, and customer satisfaction indices.

The purpose of this chapter is to organize the process of listening to the voice of the customer in such a manner that all the incoming data is reduced to a very few numbers (indices). Again, we will strive to do this in a similar manner to the financial data presentations, where a few numbers like profit margin, return on equity, and a handful of others are the primary focus of decision-making corporate managers.

THE PURPOSE OF AN INDEX

An index is a single number that, in and of itself, can give a sense of the magnitude of change in other numbers. Few people know exactly how certain indices are computed or derived, but all of us know, or have at least heard about, the more popular ones. Let's name a few for example purposes:

1. The Consumer Price Index is a single number that allows us to interpret the change in the price of millions of products/services.
2. The Dow-Jones Average is a single number that gives us an idea of how well the stock market is doing.
3. The company's overall profit margin and/or the ratio of corporate earnings to total equity—return on equity (ROE)—are indices of a company's performance.

Let's begin internally and work backwards to come up with the indices of customer satisfaction.

TRACKING INTERNAL METRICS

As we discussed in Chapter 4, to make customer relationship measurement actionable to managers, we must connect external measurements with internal, behaviorally anchored metrics. As we show in Figure 5–1, in the warranty claims business process, having very "simple paperwork" is a customer-expected attribute. This can be related to one or more internal metrics, namely the monthly number of inquiries (IM1), the monthly number of mistakes requiring resubmittal (IM2), and the monthly number of complaints

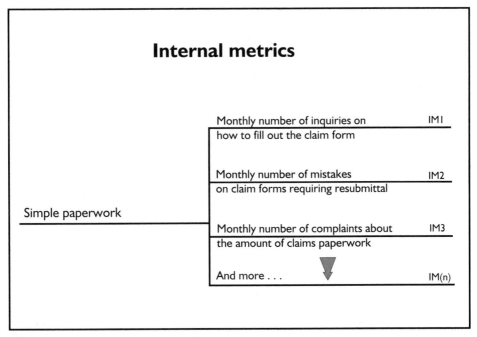

Figure 5–1. Quantifying internal metrics.

about paperwork (IM3), and more if needed. These metrics are easy to log, track, and monitor on a periodic basis.

CALCULATING INDICES

Attribute Satisfaction Index

Working backwards, we previously tied these internal metrics to the customer-expected attribute, "simple paperwork," of the warranty claims process. Then, by telephone or mail surveys we asked the customer to rate our performance on each attribute. For instance, we might ask the customer who has filed a warranty claim the following:

On a scale of 1 to 5, with 1 being strongly disagree and 5 being strongly agree, please indicate the extent to which you agree with the following statement:

"Our warranty claims paperwork is very simple to complete."

In order to turn the qualitative 1-to-5 survey scale into a grading scale based on 100 points, we normalize the data as follows:

Survey Scale	Performance Scale
1	0
2	25
3	50
4	75
5	100

Notice how this weighs more heavily the score of a 5 = 100, the delighted customer, versus 1 = 0, the very disappointed customer. This approach is in concert with our discussion in Chapter 2, Figure 2–16. Now, in order to compute an attribute satisfaction index (ASI) for each attribute tested in our survey, we add up all the performance scores for each attribute and divide by the total number of surveys to obtain the mean performance score.

In Figure 5–2, we show the customer-expected attributes for the war-

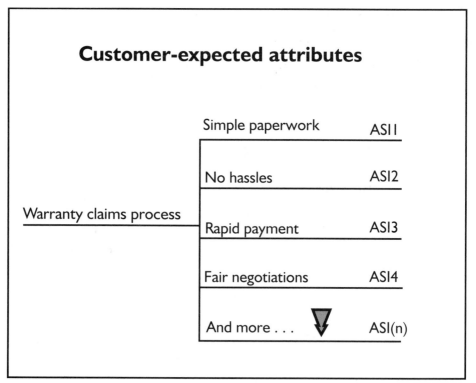

Figure 5–2. Attribute satisfaction indices.

ranty claims process, each with its own computed ASI. As we learned in Chapter 4, our performance on each attribute can be further enhanced in terms of information if we use statistics to calculate the importance, or impact, of each attribute on overall customer satisfaction.

To do this we use regression analysis (see Chapter 4 and Figures 4–10 and 4–11) and calculate an impact factor for each attribute. For now, let's give the impact factor an alphabetical name, *R*. An example of actual survey data processed into ASIs, and the calculation of *R* values is demonstrated in Chapter 7.

Process Satisfaction Index

In order to develop a quantitative picture of how the various processes that make up the company's service strategy compare, we must compute a process satisfaction index as shown in Figure 5–3. To do this, we first multiply each ASI by its statistically computed *R* value. Then we simply add all these multiple values to compute the PSI. In formula form, this would read as follows:

$$PSI_1 = (R_1)(ASI_1) + (R_2)(ASI_2) + (R_3)(ASI_3) + \ldots + (R_n)(ASI_n)$$

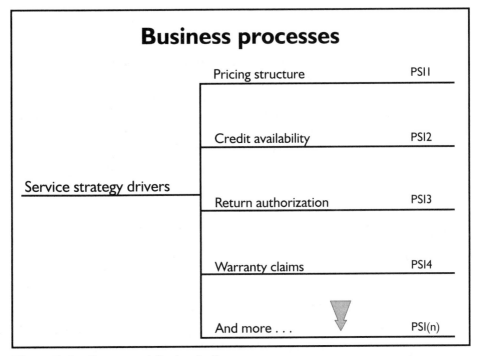

Figure 5–3. Process satisfaction indices.

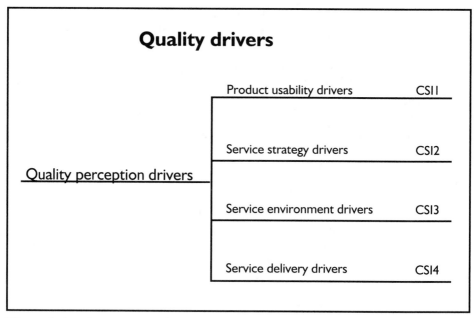

Figure 5–4. Customer satisfaction indices.

Calculating a Customer Satisfaction Index

The next step is to compute the customer satisfaction index (CSI) for each major quality driver as shown in Figure 5–4. Now we simply add all PSIs within each of the four quality drivers to compute the CSI for that driver. Finally, in Figure 5–5 the big picture of how all this very basic mathematics interacts to produce the goal stated at the beginning of the chapter, that is, to resolve all the input data to a handful, in this case four, numbers that top-management can monitor and react to for decision-making purposes.

LESSONS LEARNED

✔ Customer input data can be reduced to four key indices.

✔ Decision makers prefer to have fewer, but highly indexed numbers that indicate trends upon which to make judgments.

✔ By watching CSIs, company managers can monitor the affects that making changes to internal processes have on customer-perceived value.

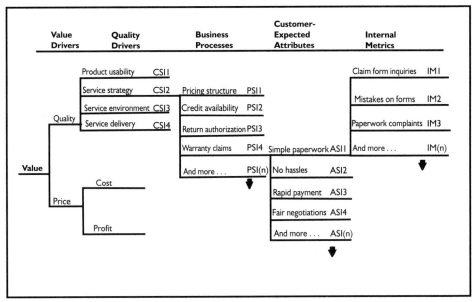

Figure 5–5. Making the quantitative connection.

✔ The best measurement tools for corporate management are those that produce financial indices, customer satisfaction indices, and market share percentages.

✔ CSIs are management's connection between varying internal metrics and customer behavior and attitudes.

6

Customer Relationship
Survey Design

INTRODUCTION

The purpose of a customer relationship survey is twofold:

- To pinpoint internal company processes with the lowest performance and the highest impact on customer retention, which therefore should be targeted for continuous improvement, or even complete re-engineering
- To create a customer relationship management tool that can be used periodically to measure continuous improvements in customer service strategies

The steps to design a customer relationship survey are as follows:

1. Establish the research team
2. Define the research statement
3. Identify all relationships
4. Identify Potential Points of Pain
5. Conduct customer interviews
6. Refine Potential Points of Pain
7. Develop a survey instrument
8. Pretest the instrument

Figure 6–1 shows the overall relationship measurement flow diagram. In this chapter we will discuss through the pretest and fielding of the survey. In

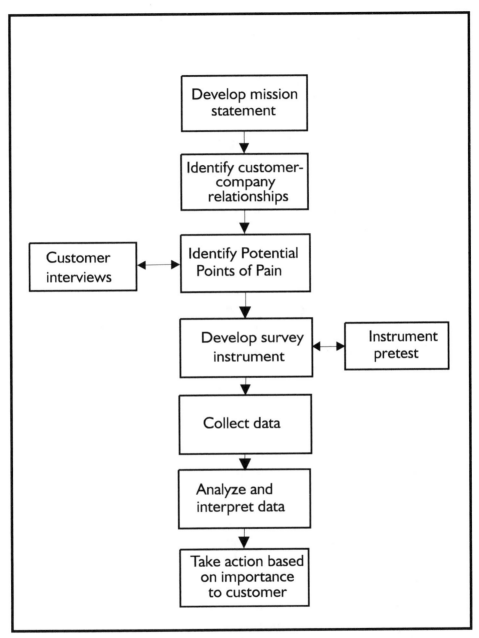

Figure 6–1. The relationship measurement process.

Chapter 7, we complete the flow chart by showing you the details of doing investigative statistical analysis of the survey data.

The skill set needed for the ideal project team can always be satisfied with a combination of individuals and talents. Team members may fulfill one or more of the needed characteristics:

1. Be an effective interviewer
2. Have analytical experience
3. Have experience with survey development
4. Have experience in statistical analysis
5. Be able to interpret numerical results
6. Be able to articulate recommendations
7. Have experience in strategic planning
8. Be an effective project manager

DEVELOPING A MISSION STATEMENT

A specific mission statement for a customer relationship survey should be agreed upon before beginning the project. It is not uncommon for a project to have too broad a scope, meaning that the researchers want to find out everything about everything with one survey. By stating the specific purpose of the survey and then focusing the qualitative and quantitative research to achieve the desired results, the project is more likely to yield actionable results for management. Keep it simple. A successful survey project will find one or two important changes to implement.

The following is an example of a mission statement for a baseline survey:

> To measure the level of customer satisfaction with the major company processes that affect the customer. Top management is committed to re-engineer the process(es) with the lowest performance and greatest impact on customer satisfaction and retention.

By including all company stakeholders in the project's mission statement, and describing the audience for the final report, the likelihood of executive action and follow-up are essentially ensured.

With the project team in place and the purpose of the research defined, you can begin the qualitative research phase. This phase will lead to the development of the survey measurement instrument or instruments.

The points of interaction between the customer and the company—

which we term the "Potential Points of Pain" related to major company processes—can be initially defined, in draft form, by the project team through intuition and experience. In addition, interviews with those managing and working in or with the major processes will uncover more customer expectations to possibly include in the survey. The following data and/or reports should be examined during the qualitative process:

1. All existing complaint compilations
2. Relevant focus group results
3. Previous surveys and results
4. Front-line employee interviews, including field personnel and call-center agents

The goal of speaking with employees is to find out where and how the customers come into contact with the company. Typical processes are order entry, warranty claims, and the toll-free customer service call center. Examining the customer complaint data will provide both insight into Potential Points of Pain as experienced by the customer and an idea of what was really expected. This initial research of the process(es) to be investigated provides a guide for the customer interviews. The actual customer interviews will test the completeness of the expectations as intuitively identified internally. These customer expectations will be the focus of the survey as we will describe in more details in later sections of this chapter.

IDENTIFYING CRITICAL RELATIONSHIPS

Most often, companies have unique relationships with different types of target customers as well as independent companies (third-party relationships) in their distribution system. Each different customer type will require a special baseline measurement, therefore requiring different survey measurement instruments.

Quite often a manufacturing company has valuable relationships with customers who are not the end-users of their products (i.e., distributors, dealers, and independent reps). Mission-critical company-to-company relationships need to be identified and subsequently monitored because the ultimate success of a company may depend totally on these other companies.

As an example, please refer to the generic relationship profile for a consumer electronics manufacturer in Figure 6–2. For the purposes of this book, we shall give this company the fictitious name of USA Electronics, Inc., and

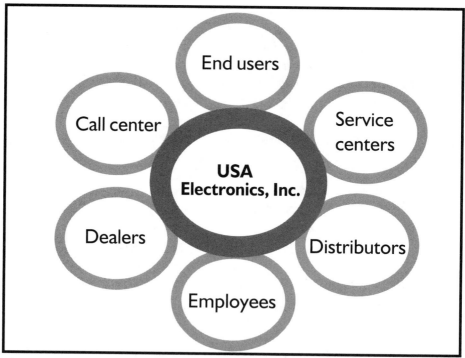

Figure 6–2. The relationship molecule.

we shall also refer to it as "USA" in later sections. In Chapter 8, USA is used in a case study of survey results.

All of the relationships shown in Figure 6–2 can have an impact on the success of the manufacturer. USA management must properly measure and manage each of the relationships shown in order to grow and prosper.

IDENTIFYING MAJOR CUSTOMER SERVICE PROCESSES

For each target customer relationship there are many Potential Points of Pain. These points are where a company interacts with its customers (both internal or external), and are the most likely opportunities where a customer can subjectively measure your company's ability to deliver to the level expected by the customer. These subjective measurements are commonly referred to as "moments of truths."

The following is a list of company processes that are most often analyzed. Most likely, some of the processes listed will be on your list, too; however, we anticipate that each company will have some unique processes as well that are not on this list.

Shipping/receiving	Warranty	Service depots
Order entry	Installation	Training
Sales	Invoicing	Collections
Technical support	Customer service	Replacement parts
Service manuals	Public relations	Communication
Services offered	Call center	Legal/contracting

FUZZY LOGIC 6.1

"Target customers will have very specific expectations before experiencing each of the above company processes, and they will acquire specific perceptions as they use your customer service strategy."

Within each of the processes there are specific customer expectations about the attributes of the process that you will need to measure. For example, in the warranty process you would include the length of the warranty, the ease of completing the paperwork needed to make a warranty claim, and the fairness in negotiating an out-of-warranty claim.

QUALITATIVE RESEARCH

The best way to get the customer involved in the design of the survey is to conduct customer interviews. However, whom should you interview? If possible, try to select customers who have experienced one or more of the major company processes and interview them about their experiences. The format of these interviews will revolve around the customer expectations of the process attributes that the internal interviews have identified. If possible, include "lost customers" among those interviewed. Lost customers are extremely valuable because they can readily identify the Points of Pain that caused them to leave the company. Plus, they have no fear of reciprocity by the company, and thus, will often "tell it like it is. . . ."

How are the customers interviewed? We have prepared the following interview guide for your review and possible adoption:

1. The main topics for discussion will center around the Potential Points of Pain that exist between a company and its customers.
2. Plan the opening statement to explain the purpose of the interview.

Assure the interview participants that their comments will be kept confidential.

3. Open-ended questions are preferred and you essentially guide the discussion with slight redirects.

4. Plan the interview questions so that you can expertly guide the discussion.

5. Plan ahead how you will record the data from each interview. It is helpful to have at least two people actively listening, so an interview team is recommended.

Recording or videotaping interviews is helpful but not always possible or appropriate for the situation. If the material needed is sensitive, the interviewee may not want his or her responses to be recorded. Be aware that recording always introduces a possible influence on the integrity of responses. In Figure 6–3 we have prepared an interview form that you may find useful.

Relationship:	Authorized Service Center
Team Members:	Name 1 Name 2
Candidates for Interview:	service managers repair specialist store manager claims processor
Method of recording:	videotape and written notes

Topics to be Covered:	background of the center's business
	who are their customers
	% of total revenue derived from your
	    company's products
	comparison to your company's competition
	two areas of relationship that need
	    immediate improvement
	dealing with your company's parts department
	ordering your company's parts
	receipt of your company's parts
	service manuals provided
	filing warranty claims
	receipt of warranty claims payment

Figure 6–3. Sample strategy outline for customer interview.

Of primary interest is to discover the major processes and the interviewee's expectations, that is, desired attributes within each major process.

Speak with all of the candidates, as outlined in your interview strategy above, at the authorized service centers. The process will be repeated at three or four other service centers in different geographic locations. Several in-person interviews are needed to develop an understanding, and then, if necessary, additional interviews can be conducted via the telephone to clarify key points of interest.

This interview procedure would be repeated for each of the relationships identified in the relationship diagram shown in Figure 6–2.

DEVELOPING THE SURVEY

With the information gathered during the customer interviews, evaluate the Potential Points of Pain that were identified during the initial internal interviews. The list may be altered by the information gathered during the qualitative research with external customers.

Review the information from the customer interviews for each relationship. The major processes are validated by observing a consistent level of agreement by the customers interviewed. Also from the interviews should come the details of the important attributes that completely describe the customers' expectations of major processes within the relationship.

To develop the survey instrument using the interview information an organizational strategy is needed. Where is the best place to start? We suggest you first make a list of the major processes of the relationship. For example, continuing with the authorized service center relationship, we have identified seven major points of interaction that a service center has with the example company. Each one becomes a process that is further defined by the customer expected attributes for that process.

For a specific example, we will continue to expand the processes between the authorized service center and USA Electronics. The details about the customers' expectations for each process gathered from the interviews should be placed into their respective process categories as shown below.

Processes	Expected Attributes
Warranty	Readily available replacement parts
	Easily identifiable part numbers
	No-hassle buybacks
	Ample length of coverage
	Minimum paperwork

Processes	Expected Attributes
Sales Tools	Effective in helping create interest
	Educational for my customers
	Differentiate me from competition
Order Entry	Orders are easy to process
	Change orders are simple
	Acknowledgments are timely
	Products can be added easily after order placed
	Order status information is available
Shipping	Packaging is thorough
	Paperwork is easy to understand
	Shipments arrive as promised
	Shipments are as ordered
Installation	Instructions are clear
	Product packaging is easy to remove
	All special tools are provided
Invoicing	Accurate
	Easy to read and understand
	Questions are answered quickly
	Payment terms are fair
	Late payment fee is normal
	Credit is appropriate
Training	Effective
	Timely
	Complete
	Available when needed

Original research done at Texas A&M University has shown that customer expectations fall into five primary categories (Zeithaml, Parasuraman, & Berry, 1990). Where possible, the format of the questions should cover these five service quality categories, which we have combined into an acronym, TERRA, meaning the good "earth" of a business process. These are explained below.

Category One: Tangibles
Definition: The physical facilities, equipment, and appearance of personnel
Installation Process Example: "Specialty tools are available to quickly and efficiently install your product at my site."

Category Two: Empathy

Definition: The caring, individualized attention provided to customers, and an understanding of their situations.

Warranty Process Example: "You accept replacement responsibilities with no hassle."

Category Three: Reliability

Definition: The ability to deliver as promised.

Shipping Process Example: "Product shipments are always delivered on or before the promised date."

Category Four: Responsiveness

Definition: The ability to assist customers in a timely fashion.

Order Entry Process Example "Order acknowledgments are sent quickly."

Category Five: Assurance

Definition: Knowledgeable employees and their ability to inspire trust and confidence.

Training Process Example: "I have complete confidence in your salesperson's advice."

Proper design of the survey instrument is extremely important to the ultimate success of the customer relationship measurement system. The data collected are only as accurate as the form and format of the questions posed. Extreme care must be taken to complete the qualitative research.

Once you complete the qualitative phase, additional care must be taken to develop a reliable, valid measurement tool. *Reliability* is an important characteristic for a survey. A reliable survey produces consistent results with respect to testing and retesting. *Validity* is also important. Validity is the extent or degree to which the survey is measuring what it is designed to measure. The final characteristic is *confidence*. A level of confidence is achieved with respect to how closely the sample approximates the population of target customers. Specifically, the number drawn for the sample must be large enough to capture the nuances of the population (customer base) so that the results can be generalized to all target customers. Typically, a confidence level of 95 percent is adequate for most situations.

DRAFTING THE SURVEY

There are common parts to every satisfaction measurement survey. Each part is important and must be included. Figure 6–4 illustrates a survey design diagram to assist you in visualizing the process under discussion.

Survey Style

We recommend using positive statements and asking for a level, or extent, of customer agreement to each statement. For example:

> On a scale of 1 to 5 with 1 being strongly disagree and 5 being strongly agree, please indicate the extent to which you agree with the following statement:
>
> "Overall, I am completely satisfied with your company."

Let's review some hints for writing good statements for your company's survey. Keep in mind the following characteristics of a good statement:

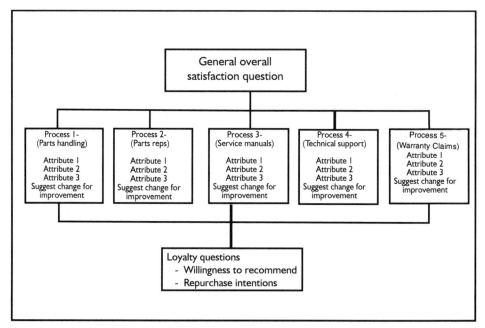

Figure 6–4.   Survey design diagram.

1. Reflects the most positive situation
2. Concise
3. Contains no ambiguity
4. Contains only one thought
5. Appears to be relevant to the "bucket" of the survey
6. Written in words familiar to the target customer

By looking at the design diagram you can see that you will need different types of statements for your company's customer satisfaction survey. We will begin with the general satisfaction question, which appears first and the questions pertaining to loyalty, which appear last. We will examine these statements first because they are similar in format.

1. Certain questions are designed to determine satisfaction with the overall relationship. There are four distinct *relationship-defining* questions:
   a. Overall satisfaction—for instance, "Overall, I am very satisfied with my relationship with your company."
   b. Willingness to repurchase—for instance, "After my experience with your company's customer information center, I am confident that your company is my choice for consumer electronics."
   c. Willingness to recommend—for instance, "I would definitely recommend your company's products to a friend."
   d. Likelihood of continued business—for instance, "Your company will definitely be one of our suppliers in five years."
   Research has shown that the question that correlates best to actual repurchase intention and brand loyalty is "willingness to recommend." These relationship-defining questions will be the dependent variables used later to derive which processes being studied have the greatest impact on customer satisfaction. The regression analysis technique used to derive impact of a process will be discussed later.
2. A second type of question is designed to specifically measure satisfaction with each expected attribute within each company process. Attributes define very specific expectations that customers have regarding Potential Points of Pain within the process being measured. These specific attributes are called "satisfaction drivers" and are used to calculate the attribute satisfaction index (ASI). ASI will be discussed in detail later.
3. A third type of question is called an open-ended question. Here the survey encourages the respondent to tell the company about something that is not covered in the survey. Research has shown that one

of the best ways to get the respondents to surface their dissatisfaction is to ask a specific question, for example, "What is one thing that our company could do to improve the warranty policy?"

4. Lastly, a well-designed survey should have the ability to categorize each respondent. Categorizing the respondent allows us to "slice and dice" the database of customer responses in different ways to discover potential trends and opportunities that may be important for management decision making. Categories might include: type of product, type of service, type of problem encountered, specific dealer type, or end-user type.

Survey Question Structure

The survey questions should be positive statements about the customer-expected attributes. Where possible and applicable we recommend you focus on the TERRA categories of service quality, namely tangibles, empathy, reliability, responsiveness, and assurance. Figure 6–5 shows several examples of questions for a call-center process.

In Figure 6–5, notice that each of the three important relationship defining statements are included. Question 1 addresses overall satisfaction. Question 7 addresses repurchase intention. Question 8 addresses recommendation

---

Examples for a company's customer information center relationship:

1. Overall, I am completely satisfied with my call to USA's Customer Information Center.
2. The toll-free number was very easy to find.
3. The customer service representative delivered on all promises made to me.
4. The customer service representative was very helpful in getting me the answer I needed.
5. The answer or solution presented to me was complete.
6. If I had another question, I would definitely call the USA customer information center.
7. My experience in contacting the USA customer information center has definitely assured me that USA is my company of choice for consumer electronic products.
8. I would definitely recommend contacting the USA customer information center to a friend in need of assistance.

Figure 6–5. Example statements for the survey.

to a friend. In a "real" survey, of course, there would be more questions included about the interaction with the customer and the information center representatives.

SELECTING SCALES FOR THE SURVEY INSTRUMENT

Survey respondents must indicate the extent of agreement with the survey statements. A 5-point scale is recommended for telephone surveys. More than 5 points becomes too difficult for the respondent to remember.

For example, "Please respond to the following statements by indicating the extent to which you agree or disagree. If you strongly disagree, say 1. If you strongly agree, say 5. If you neither agree nor disagree, say 3."

For mail surveys we recommend a 7-point scale. The respondents can easily use this scale because they have the visual benefit. Responses to a 7-point scale allow for more response variability. Statistically speaking, variability of responses is good. With the possibility for more room for a score to vary, discovering statistically significant differences is more likely.

For example, "Please respond to the following statements by indicating the extent to which you agree or disagree. If you strongly disagree, circle 1. If you strongly agree, circle 7. If you neither agree nor disagree, circle 4."

Strongly Disagree						Strongly Agree
1	2	3	4	5	6	7

For telephone surveys, a short introductory paragraph is needed. This introduction is very important because you have only a few seconds to "sell" the customer on agreeing to participate. The key components are:

1. Identification of the caller
2. The caller's affiliation
3. If applicable, the sponsor of the project
4. A brief explanation of the project
5. Positive phrase to encourage participation (may include assurance that you are not selling something)
6. Amount of time required to complete the survey

7. A promise of confidentiality
8. Verification of the phone number dialed.

Please review Figure 6–6 for an example introduction.

Anticipate objections to participation and prepare responses for common questions. The telephone survey team should be trained to effectively alleviate any concerns. Several common objections include:

1. How did you get my number?
2. How will the results of the survey be used?
3. Are my responses confidential (anonymous)?

For mail surveys, a cover letter must be included with the survey. This letter can separate or it can be placed on the inside of the cover of the survey booklet. The following are key components that should be covered within the text of the letter:

1. What the study is and why it is useful.
2. Why the respondent is important.
3. Promise of confidentiality.
4. Explanation of the identification number on the survey, if used.
5. What to do if questions arise.
6. Reward for participation, if applicable.
7. Thank you.

The cover letter should not exceed one page, as shown in the example in Figure 6–7.

The survey shown in Figure 6–8 was developed to measure the relationship that exists between USA Electronics and the authorized service center.

Hello, this is Janice from Purdue University calling on behalf of USA and I am not trying to sell anything. I am calling today to ask you a few questions about your recent call to the USA customer information center. We need your honest opinions so that USA can continually improve the service they offer to customers like yourself. This will take about 5 minutes. Your comments will be kept completely confidential. Is this 555–1212?

Figure 6–6. Example introduction.

Judy Bear
XYZ Industrial Company
Lancaster, PA

Dear Ms. Bear:

USA Electronics is working with Purdue University's Center for Customer-Driven Quality to assess the quality of USA's products and services. In order for USA to continually improve, a periodic measure of its customers' perceptions must be taken. Results from this performance assessment will be used to make the changes needed to improve USA's products and services.

Your open and honest feedback is extremely important to present a true picture of your experiences. Opinions expressed in this survey will be presented to USA in aggregate form only. Unless you specifically state that you would like your performance assessment to be shown to USA, your name will not be associated with your responses. Please note, however, that you must put your name on the survey so that we can send your participation gift.

The performance assessment will take approximately 10 minutes to complete. In advance, thank you for your willingness to share your valuable comments. Please call me should you have any questions, (317) 494–9933.

Respectfully,

Mark Gray
President
USA Electronics, Inc.

Figure 6–7. Example of cover letter.

Satisfaction Survey for
Authorized USA Service Center

Hello, this is _____ from Purdue University calling on behalf of USA Electronics, who is continuously trying to improve its relationship with authorized srvice centers. I am calling today to ask you a few questions about your experiences with USA. We need your honest opinions so that USA can continually improve the service to service centers like yours. This survey will take about 5 minutes. All information you volunteer will be kept anonymous unless you specifically indicate otherwise.

A. What percentage of your service revenue comes from USA repairs? ___ percent

Please respond to the following statements by indicating the extent to which you agree or disagree. If you strongly disagree, respond 1. If you strongly agree, respond 5. If you neither agree nor disagree, respond 3. If the statement does not apply to you or you do not know, respond 0.

	DK/NA	Strongly Disagree				Strongly Agree
1. Overall, I am completely satisfied with my relationship with USA.	0	1	2	3	4	5
2. Parts are available when I need them.	0	1	2	3	4	5
3. Parts are reasonably priced.	0	1	2	3	4	5
4. Part orders are deliveed quickly.	0	1	2	3	4	5
5. Backordered parts are delivered in a timely fashion.	0	1	2	3	4	5
6. Parts orders received are accurate.	0	1	2	3	4	5

Please suggest one improvement USA can make in handling parts: _____

7. The customer service representatives for parts orders are knowledgeable.	0	1	2	3	4	5
8. The customer service representatives for parts orders are helpful.	0	1	2	3	4	5
9. The customer service representatives for parts order are courteous.	0	1	2	3	4	5

Please make one suggestion on how USA can improve service by their parts representatives: _____

10. Service manuals for servicing products are clear.	0	1	2	3	4	5
11. Service manuals for servcing products are accurate.	0	1	2	3	4	5
12. Replacement service manuals are readily available.	0	1	2	3	4	5

Please make one suggestion on how USA can improve the service manuals:_____

(continued)

Figure 6-8. Example survey.

	DK/ NA	Strongly Disagree				Strongly Agree
13. The technical support representatives are helpful in troubleshooting defective products.	0	1	2	3	4	5
14. The technical support representatives are knowledgeable about product troubleshooting.	0	1	2	3	4	5
15. The technical support representatives are timely in helping me solve technical problems with the products	0	1	2	3	4	5

Please make one suggestion on how USA can improve service by technical support representatives:_____

16. The paperwork required to file my warranty claim is appropriate.	0	1	2	3	4	5
17. The USA warranty policy is fair.	0	1	2	3	4	5
18. USA pays my warranty claims in a timely fashion.	0	1	2	3	4	5
19. The USA warranty policy is standard for the industry.	0	1	2	3	4	5
20. The warranty claims representative is helpful.	0	1	2	3	4	5
21. The warranty calims representative is courteous.	0	1	2	3	4	5
22. The warranty claims representative is knowledgeable.	0	1	2	3	4	5

Please make one suggestion on how USA can improve the warranty policy or warranty claims handling process: _____

23. Based upon my experience with USA as an authorized service center I would recommend USA products to my friends.	0	1	2	3	4	5
24. I buy USA products for my own personal use.	0	1	2	3	4	5

Please share any other comments you may have about your relationship with USA: __

25. What is the zip code of the service center where your work? _____
Did you make any comments on this survey that you would like to further discuss with the appropriate person at USA? _____ yes
If yes, please include your name and telephone number _____   _____ no

Figure 6–8. (Continued)

SELECTING A SAMPLE

A survey sample is a statistically determined subset of the total population of target customers. This subset must be randomly selected for the survey to be valid. A sample must be large enough so that the results from the sample can be extrapolated to the entire customer group. Extrapolation is very important in producing valid results. We want to be able to say with 95 percent confidence that the whole target customer base is acting, feeling, or behaving in the same manner as the survey sample. In theory, every customer in the group should have an equal chance of being selected for the sample. If there is a list of all authorized service centers, those selected to be surveyed should be randomly selected.

A common shortcut is to sample a very small number of customers. If the sample is too small, the results will not be useful and the information that results is just "random noise" and should not be used to make business decisions. Always remember: If a survey is not methodologically sound, thereby potentially yielding invalid information, the survey project should not be conducted.

Samples are commonly drawn from two sources, namely:

- Known customers. If a customer base exists, select a random sample from that list. A customer base may be all customer contacts with the call center, or all warranty registration customers. The customers could also be all known distributors, dealers, or internal customers (employees).
- Unknown customers. When a customer base is unknown, as may be the case for companies that do not have a call center or a formal system to track their customers, a sample must be obtained from the general public. To complete a telephone survey with the general public, we recommend that you purchase a list of randomly selected telephone numbers from a commercial list company to meet your specifications. Since the customers are unknown, a qualification question must be used so that only customers who have used the product are included. For example, you might ask,

> "Have you purchased (your company's product) in the past three months?" If not, the call would be terminated.

Determining the Sample Size

Too often, the size of the sample is determined by the budget for the project. Resist the temptation to design your sample using this formula:

Total Budget/Cost per Survey = Sample Size

Instead, you must first determine the sample size needed so that the survey results will be accurate at the 95 percent confidence level, which literally means that the possibility of the results occurring by chance is only 5 percent. Is there any benefit from striving for a higher confidence level? Most often in the social sciences, the amount of time and money needed to increase the sample size to achieve a higher confidence level does not pay off in terms of better and/or different results.

Calculating the sample size required for the project is also important in determining the cost of the project. The first step is to determine the number of subgroups that you will be examining. Perhaps you want to look at customers who contacted your call center during a one month period. This is one group based on the total calls received in one-month. But, if you want to study end users who called as one group, and commercial customers who called as a second group, then a separate sample size must be calculated for each group.

$$\text{Sample size} = \frac{2500 * N * (1.96)^2}{[25(N-1)] + [2500 * (1.96)^2]}$$

N : total population (e.g., number of customer contacts, number of products registered)

As an example, let's say your company receives 20,000 customer contacts per month. If you want to complete a satisfaction survey for the customers who contacted the customer information center during a one-month period, how many completed customer surveys will you need for the results to be representative of all 20,000 contacts?

$$\text{Sample size} = \frac{2500 * 20,000 * 3.8416}{[2500 * 19,999] + [2500 * 3.8416]} = 376.939$$

So, we will need 377 completed surveys to statistically represent the 20,000 customers who contacted the call-center last month. It is important to keep in mind that the sample size needed does not increase linearly. If the number of contacts was doubled (from 20,000 to 40,000), the number of completed surveys needed does not double, as shown below:

$$\text{Sample size} = \frac{2500 * 40,000 * 3.8416}{[25 * 39,999] + [2500 * 3.8416]} = 380.52$$

The sampling pool are those customers who are selected to be contacted for the survey. The sampling pool must be larger than the statistically required sample size because all customers selected will not participate in the survey.

A general guideline for you to remember is: If your study requires 377 completed surveys (from example above), we recommend that four times that number be selected for mail surveys and two times that number be selected for a telephone survey of known customers.

A second formula that can be used is presented below. Notice that this equation does not directly account for the total population that is being examined.

Sample size = Z * Z * P * Q/D*D
   Z = confidence coefficient (1.96 for 95 percent confidence)
   P = worst score expected, usually 50 percent if nothing is known or
       if worst score expected is less than 50 percent
   Q = 1 – P
   D = confidence interval desired, usually 10 percent. D is an interval
       around a score. If the desired interval is 10 percent, there would
       be a 5 percent confidence interval on each side of the score.

Now let's look at the previous example again, namely,

Sample size = 1.96 * 1.96 * .5 * .5/.05 * .05 = 384.16

PRETESTING THE SURVEY

Trying out the survey on a small group of respondents from your sampling pool is very important. The purpose of a pretest is to

1. Determine if the questions/statements are clear
2. Determine the length of time needed for completion
3. Refine and improve the training of the survey team (for telephone)
4. Determine if any questions/statements are redundant and/or not applicable
5. Determine statistically if any questions are of minimal importance to the customers' satisfaction, or are too similar to other questions, and therefore possible candidates for elimination from the final survey instrument

FIELDING THE SURVEY

Here are our recommendations for deciding whether to use a mail or telephone format. Please refer to Figures 6-9 and 6-10 to see how cost, response rate, and the number of survey questions might alter your choice of mail versus telephone surveys.

Mail Surveys

Mail surveys are commonly used (1) when the customers are difficult to reach by phone, (2) when the project budget does not allow for telephone surveys, or (3) when the survey is too long or complicated for a telephone session.

Due to the nonresponse bias that may occur with mail surveys, saving money should not be at the expense of gathering accurate information. If a mail survey is the most appropriate for your project, build into the budget the means necessary to increase the response rate. We have found that the following actions increase response rates: (1) personalize the cover letter, (2) send precontact postcards one week early announcing the future

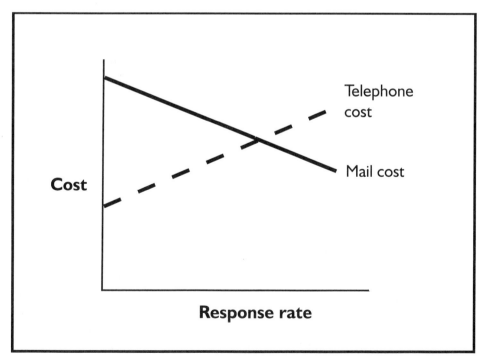

Figure 6–9. Comparing response rate to cost.

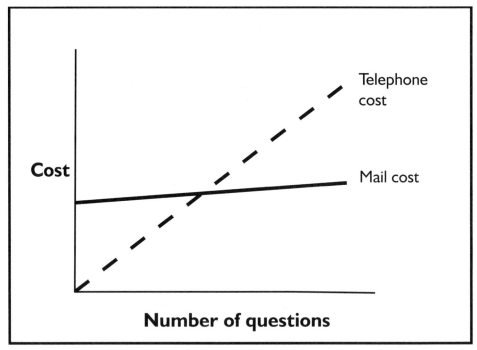

Figure 6–10. Comparing number of questions to cost.

arrival of the survey, or (3) offer an incentive for survey completion (win a product, receive coupons, or make a $1.00 or $2.00 donation to a university in the respondent's name).

For budget purposes, we recommend that you allow $5 to $10 per completed and processed survey.

Telephone Surveys

A primary benefit of the telephone survey is the ability to complete the project more quickly because the turnaround time is substantially less than when mail surveys are used. Phone surveys are often used because there is more control over the quality of the data collected. With "live" interviews, the customers have the opportunity to ask questions to further clarify a particular statement. The interviewers are thoroughly trained to respond to questions and to provide examples, if needed. Telephone surveys have considerably fewer nonrespondents and provide the opportunity to include directed open-ended questions. We recommend you budget $13 to $20 per completed and processed telephone survey. The range reflects differences in length, complexity, and timeframe for completion.

**LESSONS
LEARNED**

- ✔ Sample size is very important for producing results that are statistically representative.

- ✔ Keep survey projects focused on a specific outcome or question.

- ✔ Proper identification and measurement of the customers' Potential Points of Pain will lead to actionable results.

- ✔ The qualitative phase of the research is critical to the project's success.

- ✔ The design of the survey dictates the value of the information obtained.

Statistical Analysis of Customer Surveys

INTRODUCTION

Now that you have fielded the survey, you need to turn the raw customer response data into actionable information for management. Our purpose in survey analysis is to

1. Determine our performance on customer-expected attributes by calculating an attribute satisfaction index, ASI, for each customer expectation in each major company process.
2. Combine ASIs in each major company process to compute a process satisfaction index, PSI, for each major process.
3. Determine the impact of each PSI and ASI on overall satisfaction and repurchase.
4. Combine all the PSIs to produce one customer satisfaction index (CSI) for the company as a single metric indicating the health of customer relationships.
5. Investigate and analyze the combination of impact and performance to determine where improvements must be made to improve the customer relationship.

SELECTING A STATISTICAL PACKAGE

Many PC-based statistical packages are available. We prefer a software package called SPSS because of its ease of use, intuitive commands, and excellent technical support. We will use SPSS for Windows 6.0 for demonstration purposes in this chapter; however, the methodology would be identical for any statistical software product.

To demonstrate the analysis process of a customer relationship survey, we have created a sample data set collected for the authorized service centers of USA Electronics. The data disk to accompany this text is available on the publisher's web server. To download, begin by accessing the home page for this book:

http://www.prenhall.com

Use the search engine to locate Jon Anton, *Customer Relationship Management*. From the book home page there is a link to the downloadable file.

Let's assume the data were collected using the example survey presented earlier. We recommend you read this chapter near your PC with both SPSS and the USA data set loaded. Literally, follow along with the text and enter the SPSS commands as instructed. This will give you a "feel" for how easy it is to analyze the survey data and to produce final results.

ENTERING THE CUSTOMER SURVEY DATA

Survey Data Entry Option One

You can enter your own survey data manually into a data table, which is a spreadsheet format in SPSS. You can move around in the SPSS data table by clicking on a cell or moving the arrow keys, just like you would with any spreadsheet.

To set up a data file (Figures 7–1 through 7–4):
~ Click on **Data** in the main menu
   ~ then select **Define Variable**

~ To alter the settings click on **Type**
   ~ make sure the option for numeric is selected
   ~ click on the **Continue** button
   ~ now click on the **Label** button
   ~ name the label scheme in Variable Label:
      agrment (this name must be less than 8 characters)
   ~ with cursor in **Value,** put <u>1</u>
   ~ with cursor in **Value Label,** put <u>SD</u> (strongly disagree)
   ~ click on **Add**
   ~ repeat this process for 2 to get a value label of D, Disagree

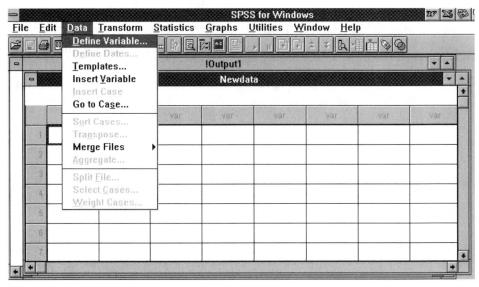

Figure 7–1.

Complete this labeling process before any data is entered. The data in the SPSS table will appear in numeric format. Later, when graphs are made from the data table, the labels will appear rather than the 1–5 ratings. Your graphs will be much more user friendly with the descriptive labels attached.

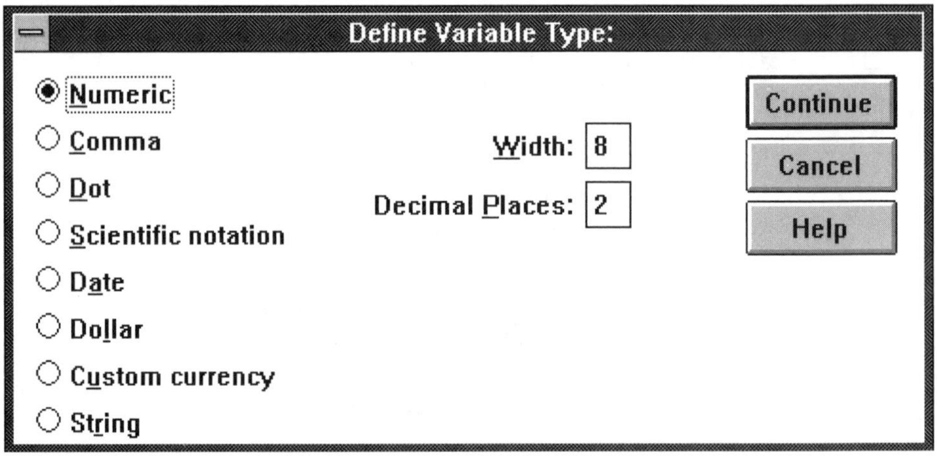

Figure 7–2.

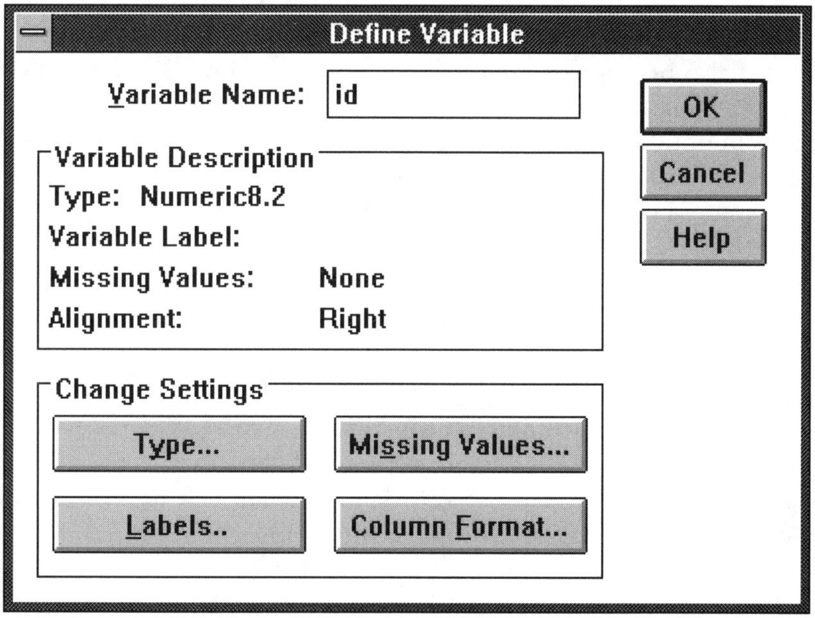

Figure 7–3.

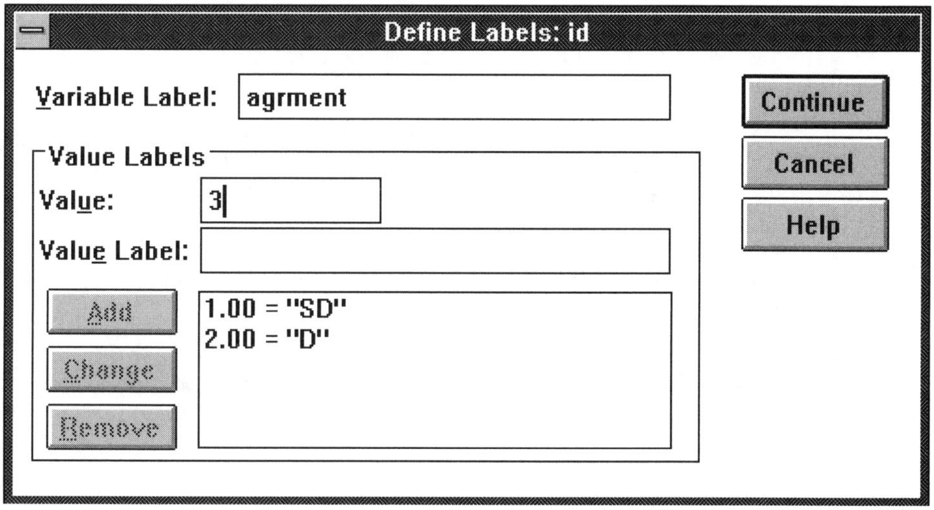

Figure 7–4.

Survey Data Entry Option Two

Data can also be imported from other sources. Using a word file, like Microsoft Word, might be easier for some users than entering data into a spreadsheet as in option one above. In a spreadsheet, the tab key or the right arrow key must be used after each cell entry. With Microsoft Word, the survey data can be entered in a continuous line with no spaces or tabs, for example, note the following sample survey data lines:

000154235415243315243321425435423152433141414244

000234152433324224155242342314232413514232344 51

000343215124231413243524354423231423345524 4332

The address for each variable is defined when it is imported. For example, columns 1–4 are reserved for the survey identification number. Column 5 is the survey answer to question 1. Column 6 is the answer to survey question 2, and so on for the rest of the data line example.

After entering your data into Word, the file must be saved in the TEXT ONLY format. Then to import this data into SPSS loaded on your PC, go to the main bar menu across the top of your screen, and

~ Select **File.**
    ~ select **Read ASCII Data**

~ Choose your text file from the list and click on the
    Define button

~ A Define Fixed Variables window will open
    ~ enter the name of your first variable into the **Name** box,
      for example, ID

~ Enter the column number where the variable begins
    in the **Start Column** box

~ Enter the column number where the variable ends in
    the **End Column** box

~ Click on the **Add** button—your first defined variable
    will appear in the **Defined Variables** box

~ Repeat this procedure by putting the next question into the **Name** box and defining the columns

~ After defining all the variables, click on the **OK** button

Now all your data will appear in the SPSS spreadsheet.

USING A DATA FILE

When all of the surveys have been entered into the file, you are ready to begin the analysis phase. To open a file, click on **File** to open and provide a name.

See Figure 7–5 for an example of what a data table looks like. Each row in the data table contains all the answers to one of your customer surveys. Each column in the data table shows the answers to a survey question. This example only shows the first nine surveys and the first fourteen questions (variables) for that survey. Notice that each survey is on its own line.

Give each survey an identification number (ID). The ID number 1 is given to the first entered survey, 2 is the second and so on. Mark the ID

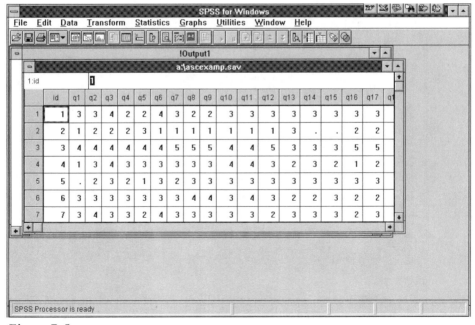

Figure 7–5.

number assigned on the corresponding survey. You may find a need to refer
back to a survey to fix a data entry error. If ID numbers are not on the surveys, it becomes extremely difficult to find and to fix a data entry error.

INVESTIGATING THE AGGREGATE SAMPLE OF SURVEYS

A natural place to begin is to ask the question "How did the total sample respond to each question?" The results are generally presented in the from of a
table or graph of the frequency of answers to each question, called a frequency report. The frequency of response is the total number of respondents
who gave the same answer to a specific question.

To demonstrate how easy this analysis process is, let's request a frequency
report on a specific question. First, click on **Statistics** then **Frequencies,** as
shown in Figure 7–6.

As an example, we will look at question 3 from our survey. The question
asked for agreement on the statement "Parts are reasonably priced." Once

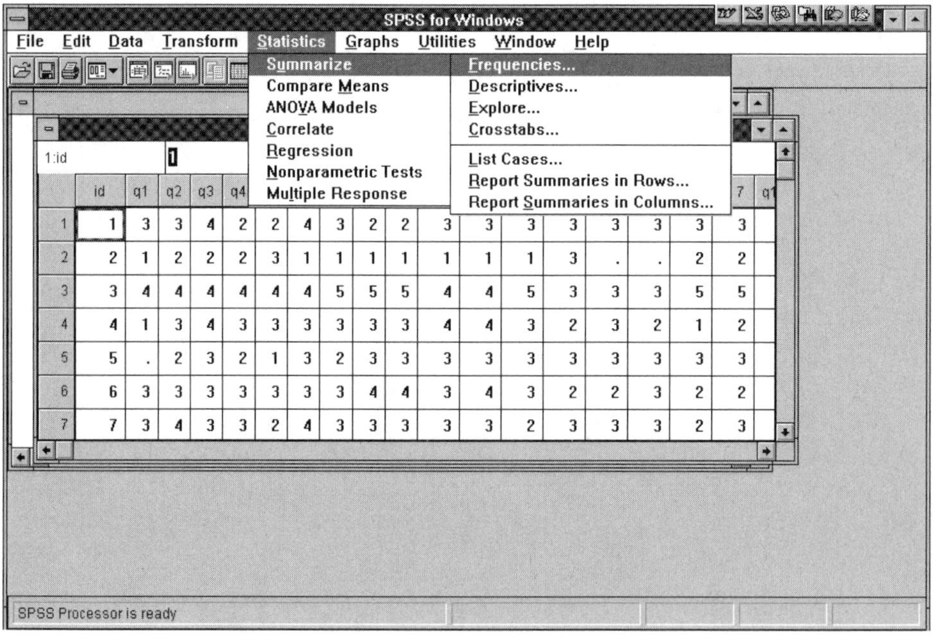

Figure 7–6.

the **Frequencies** window is open, you will see a list of all of the questions on the left (Figure 7–7). All of the questions (variables) are listed in this box. Notice the scroll bar that is on the right side (vertical) of the variables box. You can scroll through the list by clicking on the scroll bar. The questions are ordered by their first digit, then the second digit. All of the variables beginning with 1 are at the top of the list. After 1–9 is 2, then 2–0 then 2–1.

You can highlight a question for analysis from the list. When the question of interest has been selected (highlighted), click on the right arrow button to put it into the **Variable(s)** list. When you have transferred the variable of interest, click on **OK** and the frequency will be generated. (Note: You may want to look at the responses for all of the questions so you can highlight the list and click on the right arrow to move them all into the **Variables** box.)

Figure 7–8 is an example of how the output will appear in the output window. The Frequency column is an exact count of how many survey participants responded with each level of agreement to the statement. For example, 240 individuals said that they "Agreed" with the statement. The next column, Percent, indicates that 240 is 39.7 percent of all who answered that question.

For your investigation, and presentation of results, it can be important to graph the responses to each question. You might use a bar chart or pie chart to display the frequency of customer responses.

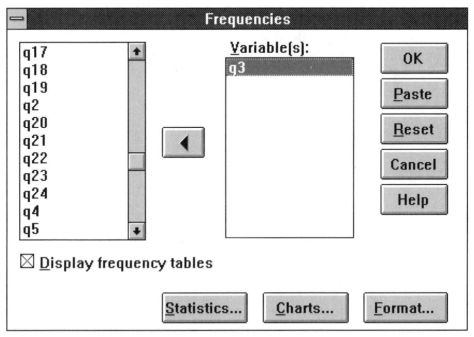

Figure 7–7.

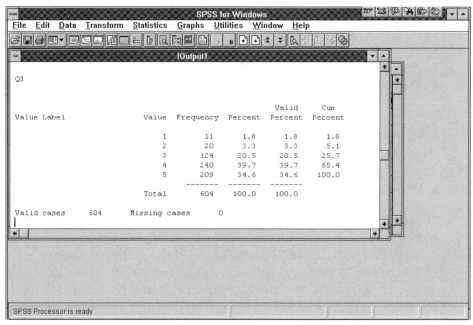

Figure 7–8.

To make a bar chart (Figure 7–9)

~ Click on **Graphs** in the main menu
   ~ then select **Bar** from the list of choices
   ~ select the survey question of interest by clicking on it
   ~ click on the right arrow to move it to the X-axis box
   ~ click on the **OK** button

The characteristics of the chart can be altered by selecting from the options that appear directly above the graph. For example, if you select the crayon symbol you can alter the color. If you click on the silhouette of a bar chart, you can alter the appearance.

PREPARING THE DATA

To monitor progress over time, a number that summarizes performance must be calculated. Your customer relationship survey will establish a baseline against which future measurements can be compared.

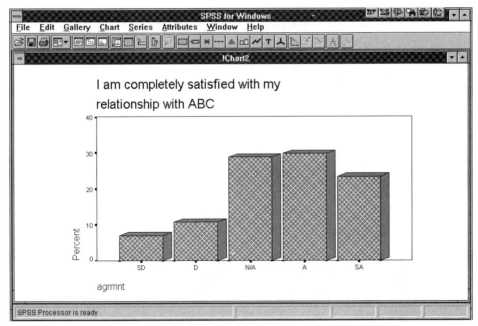

Figure 7–9.

Calculating the indices will begin at the lowest level with the attributes of the process, that is, Attribute Satisfaction Index (ASI). Unfortunately, we cannot simply generate a mean for each attribute to produce the ASI. How to prepare the data is explained below.

When means are calculated, all of the responses to the question are summed and then the total is divided by the number of respondents. The problem arises when someone responds with a zero because the attribute does not apply to them. So, a zero is added to the total. The total number is then divided by the number of respondents. A zero did not add anything to the total but that person is still included in the denominator.

$$\text{Mean} = \frac{X_1 + X_2 + X_3 + X_4 + X_5}{5} = \frac{3 + 4 + 2 + 5 + 4}{5} = 3.6$$

But if someone responded "does not apply" a zero is recorded:

$$\text{Mean} = \frac{3 + 4 + 2 + 0 + 4}{5} = 2.6$$

For this reason, we normalize the data by recoding it as follows:

Response		Normalized Response
5	=	100
4	=	75
3	=	50
2	=	25
1	=	0
0	=	50*

*If the situation does not apply, the zero value is recoded as 50. By assigning the midpoint value, the mean will not be influenced.

To re-code the data in your file (Figure 7–10):

~ Click on **Transform** in the main menu
   ~ select **Recode,** then **Into Different Variables**
   ~ highlight the survey question of interest
   ~ click on the right arrow to move it to the
      Numeric Variable → Output Variable box
   ~ give variable a new name in the **Output
      Variable Name** box (change q1 → q1m)
   ~ click on **Change** button
   ~ click on the **Old and New Values** button

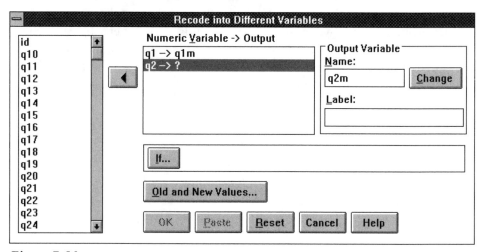

Figure 7–10.

The **Old and New Values** window will open (Figure 7–11). Here is where you define the new values.

Enter a value in the **Old Value box** (where there is now a 5). In the **New Value** box place the reassigned value, which is 100 in this example. Then click on the **Add** button and the recoded value will appear in the **Old → New** box. In the example below the values for 1, 2, 3, 4, and missing have been added to the box.

Click on the **Continue** button and you will be returned to the screen that appears in Figure 7–11. Repeat the same procedure for q2. You will not have to go through the defining of the six values, but rather they will appear as defined by the last variable and you simply click on the **Continue** button to accept them for this variable.

Once you have recoded all of the variables, click on the **OK** button, which is under the **Old and New Values** button. The new variables created will appear in columns that immediately follow your last variable in the original data file. The new variables will appear with the recoded values (Figure 7–12). These new variables will be used to calculate the ASIs and PSIs, which are discussed in the next sections.

Then you may want to examine the frequencies using the normalized data in a bar chart (Figure 7–13).

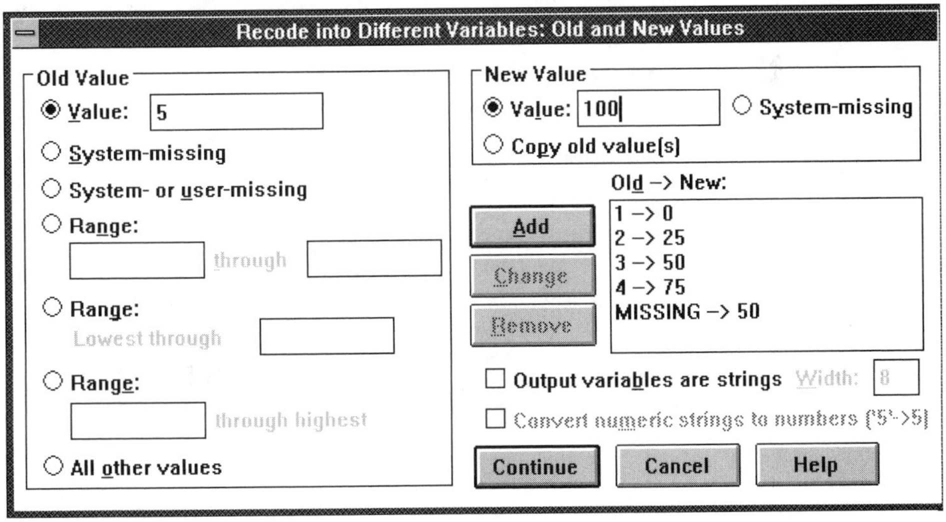

Figure 7–11.

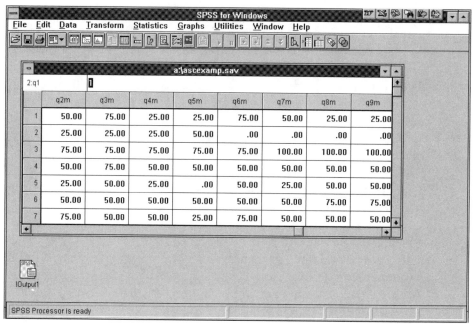

Figure 7–12.

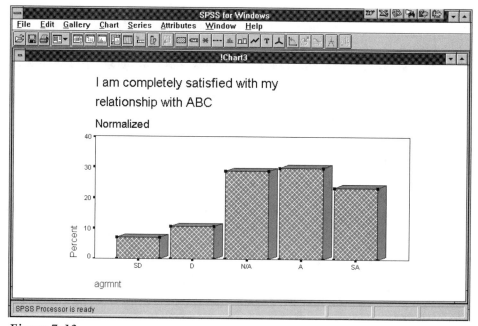

Figure 7–13.

DEFINING THE MAJOR PROCESSES

The next step in your analysis is to set up the strategy to determine the performance level for each of the major processes. The process means will be calculated by creating a subscale using the attributes that comprise that process. Let's look at the survey to clearly understand what you need to do in this step.

Please refer to the USA Electronics authorized service center survey in Figure 6–8. The processes being researched are grouped clearly with an open-ended question at the end. For example, numbers 2, 3, 4, 5, and 6 define the process of Parts Handling. Numbers 7, 8, and 9 define the process of Parts Representatives. The questions for each process will be converted into a scale using the normalized data.

To construct the process variables (Figure 7–14):
  ~ Click on **Transform** in the main menu
    ~ select **Compute** from the pull-down menu
    ~ in the **Compute Variable** window, name the **Target Variable** (in example, "Parts" because it is the process being defined)
    ~ select the ( ) on the keypad. The parentheses will appear in the **Numeric Expression** box. Put the cursor between the two and add a few spaces.

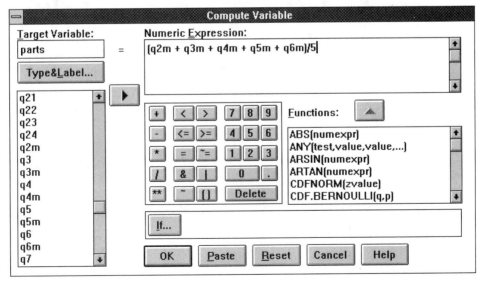

Figure 7–14.

~ select the question from the question list and click on the right
    arrow button. The question will be moved into the parentheses.
~ select the **+** from the keypad
~ select the next question and select a **+**. Repeat until all questions
    needed are in the parentheses.
~ select the division symbol (**/**) from the keypad
~ select the total number of questions used for the process
~ click on the **OK** button

CALCULATING MEANS
OF THE NORMALIZED DATA

Now you are ready to calculate the Attribute means (ASI). To calculate a
mean, click on **Statistics** in the main menu and select **Descriptives** from the
pull-down menu. A Descriptives box will open (Figure 7–15). Select the
questions and process variables of interest by highlighting them and clicking
on the right arrow button to move them to the **Variable(s)** list. You need to
find the means for all of the questions and all of the process scales that you
created. When all have been moved over, click on the **OK** button.

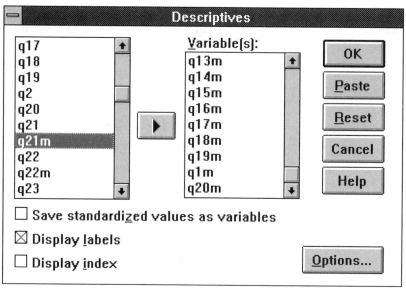

Figure 7–15.

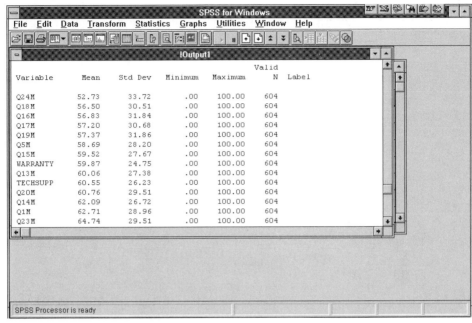

Figure 7–16.

	SPSS for Windows					
File Edit Data Transform Statistics Graphs Utilities Window Help						

IOutput1

Variable	Mean	Std Dev	Minimum	Maximum	Valid N	Label
Q24M	52.73	33.72	.00	100.00	604	
Q18M	56.50	30.51	.00	100.00	604	
Q16M	56.83	31.84	.00	100.00	604	
Q17M	57.20	30.68	.00	100.00	604	
Q19M	57.37	31.86	.00	100.00	604	
Q5M	58.69	28.20	.00	100.00	604	
Q15M	59.52	27.67	.00	100.00	604	
WARRANTY	59.87	24.75	.00	100.00	604	
Q13M	60.06	27.38	.00	100.00	604	
TECHSUPP	60.55	26.23	.00	100.00	604	
Q20M	60.76	29.51	.00	100.00	604	
Q14M	62.09	26.72	.00	100.00	604	
Q1M	62.71	28.96	.00	100.00	604	
Q23M	64.74	29.51	.00	100.00	604	

SPSS Processor is ready

Figure 7–16.

	SPSS for Windows					
File Edit Data Transform Statistics Graphs Utilities Window Help						

IOutput1

Q23M	64.74	29.51	.00	100.00	604
Q21M	64.98	29.17	.00	100.00	604
Q22M	65.44	26.91	.00	100.00	604
Q4M	68.83	26.04	.00	100.00	604
Q2M	69.08	25.04	.00	100.00	604
PARTS	69.52	20.71	.00	100.00	604
Q7M	69.83	24.58	.00	100.00	604
Q8M	70.61	25.98	.00	100.00	604
Q10M	70.82	26.04	.00	100.00	604
PARTSREP	70.96	24.14	.00	100.00	604
Q12M	71.03	25.41	.00	100.00	604
SERVMAN	71.18	22.62	.00	100.00	604
Q11M	71.69	24.34	.00	100.00	604
Q9M	72.43	26.81	.00	100.00	604
Q3M	75.50	23.03	.00	100.00	604
Q6M	75.50	24.04	.00	100.00	604

SPSS Processor is ready

Figure 7–17.

TABLE 7–1.　　Performance Metrics for the Authorized Service Centers

		PSIs	ASIs	
Authorized service centers ____	Parts handling ____		Availability	**69.08**
			Reasonably priced	**75.50**
			Delivered quickly	**68.83**
			Timely delivery	**58.69**
			Accuracy	**75.50**
	Parts reps ____		Knowledgeable	**69.83**
			Helpful	**70.61**
			Courteous	**72.43**
	Service manuals ____		Clear	**70.82**
			Accurate	**71.69**
			Available	**71.03**
	Tech support ____		Helpful	**60.06**
			Knowledgeable	**62.09**
			Timely	**59.52**
	Warranty claims ____		Appropriate paperwork	**56.83**
			Fair	**57.20**
			Timely payment	**56.50**
			Industry standard	**57.37**
			Helpful reps	**60.76**
			Courteous reps	**64.98**
			Knowledgeable reps	**65.44**

The output window will display the descriptive statistics, as shown in Figures 7–16 and 7–17. Now the means of the normalized data can be used to establish a metric for performance on the attribute characteristics that can be monitored over time. The ASI values should be placed into the Performance Metrics Table (Table 7–1). We will calculate the Process Satisfaction Index (PSI) after completing the regression analysis. This display would be repeated for each of the other relationships measured.

HOW PERFORMANCE IMPACTS SATISFACTION

You have already calculated the performance of USA Electronics, Inc. with respect to the attributes and processes with the means. Calculating the impact of an attribute or process on overall satisfaction is a little more complicated. Regression analysis enables you to empirically demonstrate the amount of impact each process has on overall customer satisfaction with the company.

To understand what regression analysis does, picture this regression equation:

Overall satisfaction with USA = f(handling of parts, parts representatives, service manuals, warranty claims, technical service representatives)

In words, overall satisfaction with USA is a function of handling of parts, parts representatives, and so on. This statement makes sense because one would expect these processes to contribute to satisfaction. If you would decide to include the process of installation, that would not make sense when examining Authorized Service Centers. The regression equation with the processes should be written out and make sense before the first survey is even sent to a customer. Regression analysis enables you to statistically determine the impact of each of those processes on overall satisfaction, as well as on willingness to recommend, and on repurchase intention.

How does regression analysis do that? Picture a multidimensional space called "overall satisfaction." All of the data points for the attributes are positioned in this space with respect to the customers' responses. Regression fits the best line through the data. The best line means that the amount of distance between the line and all of the data points is the smallest, the smallest amount of error. See the Figure 7–18 for a two-dimensional representation of the regression procedure.

The positioning of this line in the space is impacted by the variables. Picture the line tilting because of the impact of a variable. The variables that have the greatest impact on the line are the ones we are interested in because they are having an impact in this space called "overall satisfaction."

To conduct a regression analysis (Figure 7–19):
~ Click on **Statistics** in the main menu
  ~ select **Regression** from the pull-down menu
  ~ select **Linear** from the sub-menu

The variables that are selected first for the regression analysis are the process variables. We want to examine how much each process is impacting the dependent variable. The dependent variable in this example is overall satisfaction (q_1). Each of the processes is placed into the Independent variable box. Three of the processes are visible in the box in the example below: service manuals, technical support, and warranty policy/warranty claims. The two remaining processes are hidden in that box: parts handling and parts representatives (Figure 7–20).

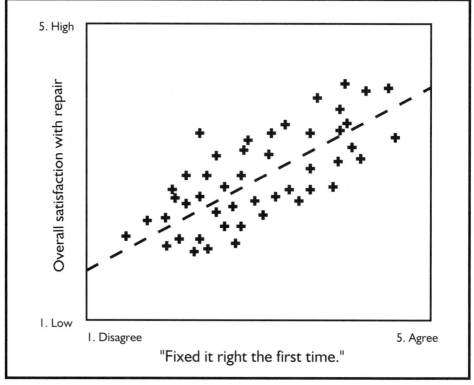

Figure 7–18.   Attribute impact diagram.

So we are testing

q_1 = f(parts, parts reps, tech support, service manuals, warranty)

The different methods for regression analysis are entry, stepwise, remove, backward, and forward. These methods dictate how the variables enter the regression equation. The two most commonly used methods are entry and stepwise.

After selecting the variables, click on **OK.** The output will appear as in Figure 7–21.

Of interest in the first page of output is the *R*-square value in Figure 7–21. In this example, *R*-square equals .557, which means that 55.7 percent of the variance in overall satisfaction ratings is explained by the processes that are included in the model. In the social sciences, an *R*-square value in excess of .4000 is considered to indicate a good model.

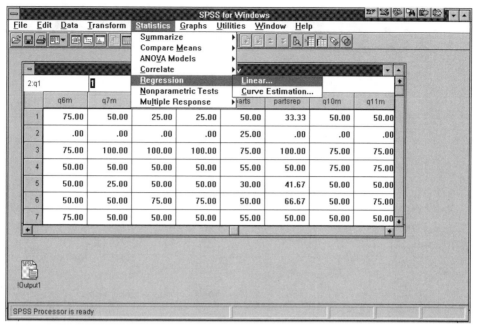

Figure 7–19.

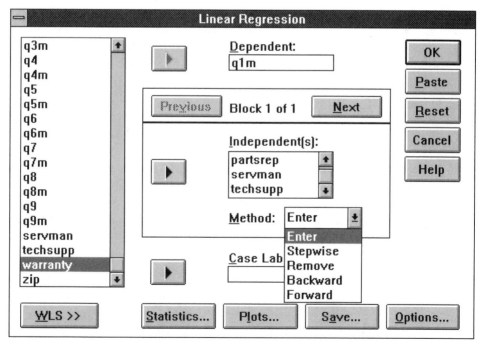

Figure 7–20.

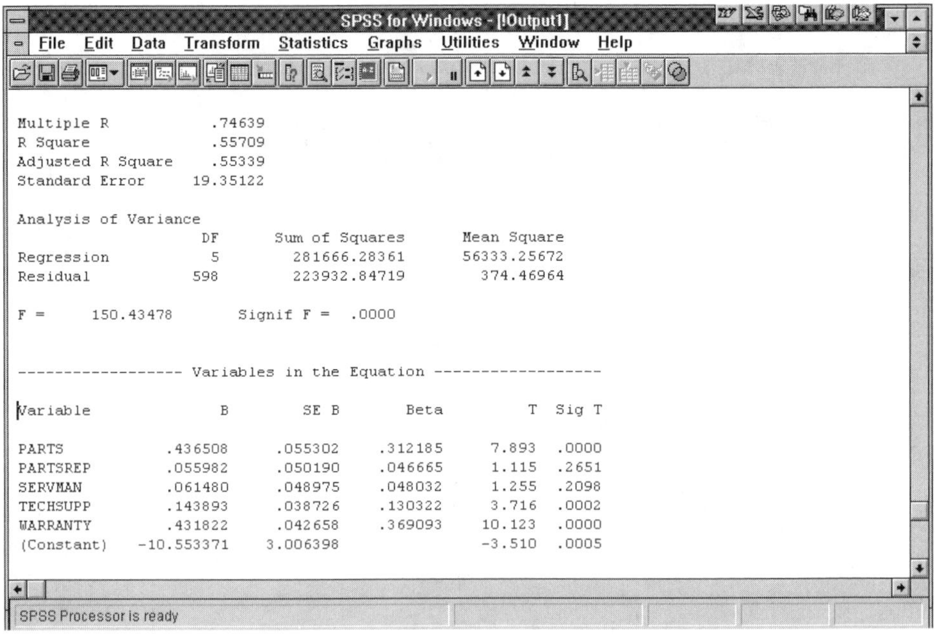

Figure 7–21.

Look at the significance of *F*. If *F* is greater than .05, then the model is not adequately explaining overall satisfaction. The impact of each independent variable (process) is evident in the *B* value (see Figure 7–21). This coefficient will be used to evaluate the impact of that process. Notice in the far right column is the significance of *T* (Sig T). Each of the processes should have a significant *T*-value, a value that is less than .05.

In the column marked "B" are the values used to determine impact. Notice that parts and warranty are the two processes that are influencing overall satisfaction the most because the values are the largest. Knowing that parts and warranty are having the greatest impact does not allow you to recommend specific things to focus on for improvement. You must conduct a regression analysis using the attributes that make up parts and for the attributes that make up warranty.

$$q_1 = f(q_2 \ q_3 \ q_4 \ q_5 \ q_6), \text{ and}$$

$$q_1 = f(q_{16} \ q_{17} \ q_{18} \ q_{19} \ q_{20} \ q_{21} \ q_{22})$$

The regression procedure is set up exactly as demonstrated above, except the independent variables are changed. The output appears in Figure 7–22.

```
┌─────────────────────────────────────────────────────────────────────────┐
│ ▒▒▒▒▒▒▒▒▒▒▒▒▒▒▒▒▒▒▒ SPSS for Windows - [!Output!] ▒▒▒▒▒▒▒  ▦ ░ ▦ ▦ ░ ░ ▾ ▴│
│ ▫ File  Edit  Data  Transform  Statistics  Graphs  Utilities  Window  Help ▾│
│ ▦▦▦▦▾ ▦▦▦▦▦▦ ▦ ▦▦▦▦ ▦  ▮ ▦▦▦ ▦ ▦ ▦▦▦▦ ▦▦                                   ▴│
│                                                                            │
│ Multiple R          .64471                                                 │
│ R Square            .41565                                                 │
│ Adjusted R Square   .41077                                                 │
│ Standard Error    22.22733                                                 │
│                                                                            │
│ Analysis of Variance                                                       │
│                   DF      Sum of Squares      Mean Square                  │
│ Regression         5        210154.65182     42030.93036                   │
│ Residual         598        295444.47897       494.05431                   │
│                                                                            │
│ F =      85.07350       Signif F =  .0000                                  │
│                                                                            │
│                                                                            │
│ ------------------ Variables in the Equation ------------------            │
│                                                                            │
│ Variable            B         SE B       Beta        T    Sig T            │
│                                                                            │
│ Q2M             .439899     .059992    .380469    7.333   .0000            │
│ Q3M             .029718     .055038    .023637     .540   .5894            │
│ Q4M             .116911     .061207    .105138    1.910   .0566            │
│ Q5M             .079609     .047565    .077516    1.674   .0947            │
│ Q6M             .201086     .046594    .166972    4.316   .0000            │
│ (Constant)     2.173561    3.483089                .624   .5328            │
│                                                                            │
│ SPSS Processor is ready                                                     │
└─────────────────────────────────────────────────────────────────────────┘
```

Figure 7–22.

From the analysis, it now becomes evident that number 2 (parts availability) and number 6 (accuracy of parts orders) are the attributes that should be the target for re-engineering.

The regression analysis is completed for the attributes comprising the second most important process, warranty claims. The results presented in Figure 7–23 indicate that numbers 16 (paperwork), 17 (fairness of warranty policy), 19 (industry standard policy), and 22 (knowledge of the warranty claims reps) should be the targets for re-engineering.

To visually represent the impact of each process, it is helpful to put the impact value and the performance value on the same chart (Table 7–2).

The information in this table can be graphically displayed for maximum effectiveness. This will be shown in detail in Chapter 8.

Let's revisit the regression equation. First in scientific language:

$$Y = \text{intercept} + B_1X_1 + B_2X_2 + B_3X_3 + B_4X_4 + B_5X_5$$

Since we have solved for B, or impact, the values can be substituted:

$$Y = \text{intercept} + .369X_1 + .312X_2 + .130X_3 + .048X_4 + .047X_5$$

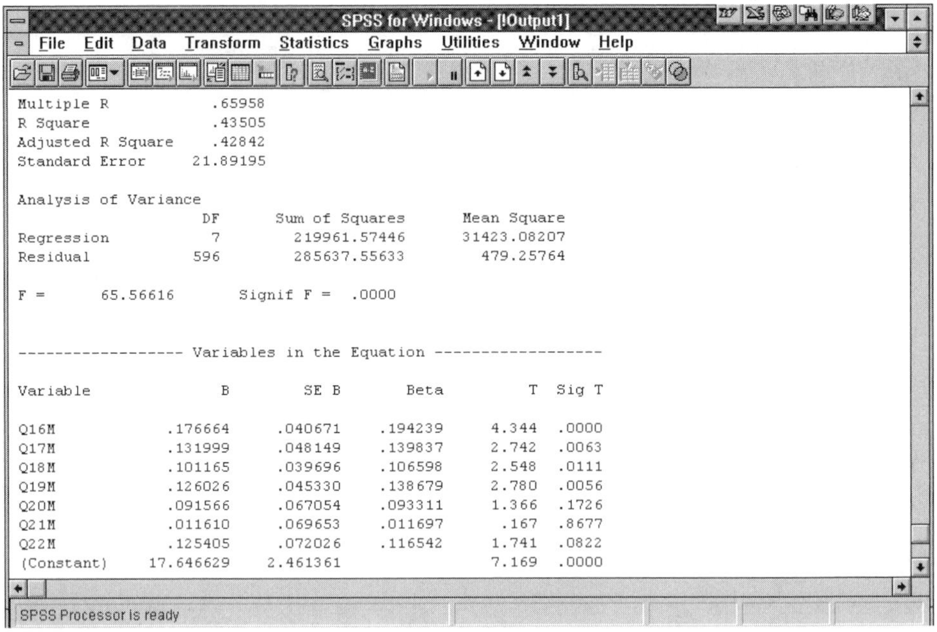

Figure 7–23.

If you revisit the verbal regression equation presented in the beginning of this section, the general theme of regression should be more clear. Each X in the equation is a process presented in the order that it appears in Table 7–2. How the consumer responded to the performance of that process times the impact plus the other processes times their impacts predicts their overall satisfaction rating.

Overall satisfaction with USA = f(handling of parts, parts representatives, service manuals, warranty claims, technical service representatives)

TABLE 7–2. **Impact and Performance Values**

	Impact (B)	*Performance*
1. Warranty policy/warranty claims	.369	59.07
2. Parts handling	.312	69.52
3. Technical support reps	.130	60.55
4. Service manuals	.048	71.18
5. Parts representatives	.047	70.96

CALCULATING THE PSIs

The attribute satisfaction indices were calculated earlier. The Process Satisfaction Indices (PSI) are calculated last because the impact values from the regression analysis are used.

By doing the regression analysis, you saw how the different attributes had varying degrees of impact on overall satisfaction. It is for that reason that the attributes are weighted based on their respective impacts when calculating the PSI (Table 7–3). The same procedure would be repeated for each of the remaining processes. The totals for each of the processes should be placed into the Performance Metrics Table shown in Table 7–4.

To calculate the overall performance for USA's authorized service center, repeat the procedure using impact and performance of the process instead of the individual attributes (Table 7–5).

CALCULATING THE COMPANY'S CSI

We have worked through the analysis for the authorized service center survey. USA Electronics has other important relationships that would be measured, such as with distributors and end users (see Figure 6–2.) These relationships would involve different process, but the method of analysis outline in this chapter would yield an overall performance value as shown in Table 7–4. This overall performance rating would be added for all relationships

TABLE 7–3.   **Impact Performance**

	Impact (B)	Performance	Impact times Performance
1. Availability of parts	.380	69.08	26.25
2. Parts are reasonably priced	.024	75.50	1.81
3. Parts orders are delivered quickly	.105	68.83	7.23
4. Back-orders delivered in timely fashion	.078	58.69	4.58
5. Parts orders are accurate	.167	75.50	12.61
		Total:	52.48

TABLE 7–4.   Performance Metrics for the Authorized Service Centers

	PSIs	ASIs	
		Availability	**69.08**
		Reasonably priced	**75.50**
	Parts handling	Delivered quickly	**68.83**
	52.48	Timely delivery	**58.69**
		Accuracy	**75.50**
		Knowledgeable	**69.83**
	Parts reps	Helpful	**70.61**
	_____	Courteous	**72.43**
Authorized		Clear	**70.82**
service	Service manuals	Accurate	**71.69**
centers	_____	Available	**71.03**
58.41		Helpful	**60.06**
	Tech support	Knowledgeable	**62.09**
	_____	Timely	**59.52**
		Appropriate paperwork	**56.83**
		Fair	**57.20**
		Timely payment	**56.50**
	Warranty claims	Industry standard	**57.37**
	_____	Helpful reps	**60.76**
		Courteous rep	**64.98**
		Knowledgeable rep	**65.44**

TABLE 7–5.   Impact Performance

	Impact *(B)*	*Performance*	*Impact times* *Performance*
1. Warranty policy/ warranty claims	.369	59.07	22.09
2. Parts handling	.312	69.52	21.69
3. Technical support reps	.130	60.55	7.87
4. Service manuals	.048	71.18	3.42
5. Parts representatives	.047	70.96	3.34
		Total:	58.41

measured. Find the mean of these number to arrive at an overall customer satisfaction index (CSI) as discussed in Chapter 5.

The value of the CSI should be rounded to no fewer than four decimal places. Avoid unnecessary rounding of numbers because over time that may cause the CSI value to fluctuate.

LESSONS LEARNED

✔ Descriptive statistics, like frequencies, allow you to see only how the sample responded to each question, and therefore, does not yield actionable information.

✔ ASIs allows you to assess performance with respect to the customer-expected attributes within a process.

✔ Regression analysis enables you to empirically determine the impact (or importance) of the attribute and processes to customer satisfaction.

✔ PSIs are generated by multiplying the ASI by its respective impact factor or weight.

8

Using Customer Relationship Survey Results

INTRODUCTION

In the last two chapters, we have been using USA Electronics, Inc. as our example company for designing, fielding, and statistically analyzing a survey. The objective of this chapter is to push back and look at USA Electronics as a business case study and demonstrate how a manager might implement techniques we've described to produce actionable information about customer relationships. This exercise is partly to prepare the reader for the five additional business cases discussed in Chapter 10. Let's review the background of USA Electronics (also called USA) and give it some personality. As mentioned earlier, this is a real business case, with real people, but we have been very careful to change the names to "protect the innocent."

CASE OVERVIEW

USA Electronics is a leading manufacturer in the highly competitive industry of consumer electronics. Foreign companies dominate certain segments of the market and are threatening to go after the USA customer base as well. Excellent customer service and technical support have helped USA maintain its market position.

The company sells its products through both large and small retailers, very few of which actually have the ability to repair the USA product either during or after the warranty period. Instead, USA Electronics selects small, independent electronics service shops who want to handle the USA product, and then trains their technicians to do the repairs. In order to become an official authorized USA service center, the servicer must be certified by USA to have the proper technical skills and test equipment to fix the products quickly and professionally.

Jerry Wordell has just been appointed the National Service Manager. During the first month in his new job, Jerry reviews the company's complaint logs and finds that a rather high number of complaints have been received from end-users, (customers actually using USA's products). The complaints are almost all about the poor service received from the USA authorized service centers. Since the service centers are a very critical component in USA's service strategy, Jerry knows that customer-perceived value can easily be affected, and market damage could quickly follow.

Jerry decides to develop two separate surveys to measure the relationship between USA and its 1,364 authorized service centers, and to measure the relationship between USA's authorized service centers and the USA customers that have had their USA product serviced recently. For purposes of this chapter, we will focus only on the results of the first survey.

SURVEY DESIGN AND IMPLEMENTATION

In Chapter 6 we have already stepped through the design and testing of USA's survey, which you should review briefly in Figure 6–8. From the survey questions, you can see that the major processes of USA that affect an authorized service center are as follows:

Questions	Process
1. 2, 3, 4, 5, and 6	Parts handling
2. 7, 8, and 9	Parts representative
3. 16, 17, 18, 19, 20, 21, and 22	Warranty claims
4. 13, 14, and 15	Technical support
5. 10, 11, and 12	Service manuals

Jerry decided to use the telephone for his survey in order to get the results quickly and also to obtain some additional qualitative "input" from the servicers through the open-ended questions.

In Chapter 7, we showed how the survey data from each respondent is entered into SPSS, and how to navigate through SPSS to obtain the necessary statistics for investigation and analysis.

FROM DATA TO MANAGEMENT INFORMATION

The detailed statistical steps of Chapter 7 are very important; however, because of the complexity, little of the data or reports are appropriate for management's review and/or decisions. In order to better convert the statistical data into management information, we take the numbers from the regression analysis and the PSI and ASI ratings and plot them in the horizontal impact/performance bar chart shown in Figure 8–1. In order to produce this figure, the SPSS results were ported to Corel Draw, a popular presentation software package.

Let's demonstrate how much easier it is to interpret graphically represented information. The following are some observations that we can make from this bar chart:

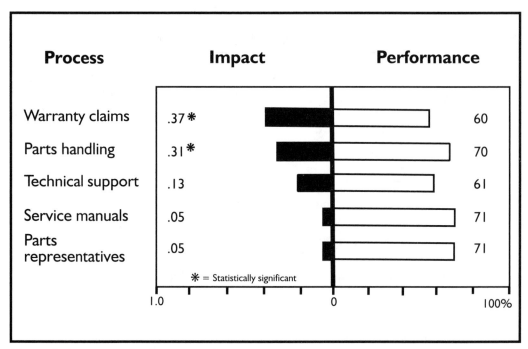

Figure 8–1.   Impact/performance of major processes.

1. Warranty claims and parts handling both have a statistically significant impact on servicer satisfaction with USA Electronics.
2. Notice how USA's performance is the lowest in warranty claims processing, yet to the service center managers, this process has the highest impact on their satisfaction.
3. Notice how USA's performance in service manuals and parts representative is the highest, however, the impact (importance) of these processes on the servicers' satisfaction is not statistically significant.

In order to further investigate each of the significant processes, we can "drill down" and graph the customer-expected attributes in each process. These are shown in Figures 8–2, and 8–3. In each bar chart two issues become immediately obvious—which attribute is significantly affecting satisfaction and USA's performance on each important attribute.

The management value of the bar charts shown above can be further enhanced by transposing the data onto a decision matrix as shown in Figure 8–4, previously discussed in Chapter 4. The challenge depicted in this figure is to move those processes in which the company scores low, but that have high impact, into the "top box," that is, the upper right box. This will prob-

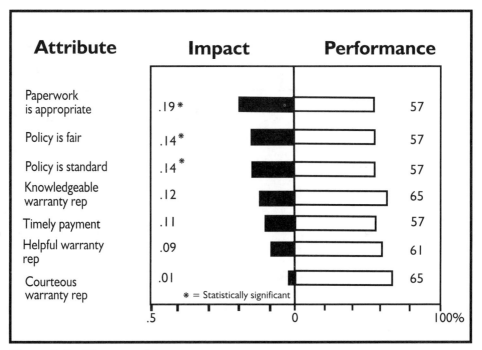

Figure 8–2. Warranty claims process.

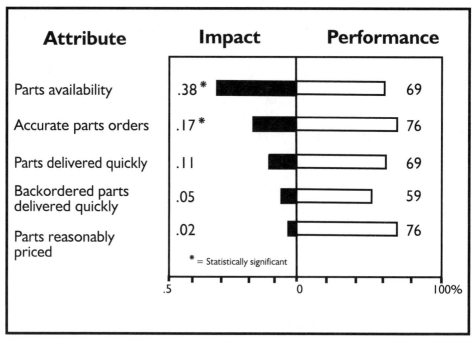

Figure 8–3. Parts handling process.

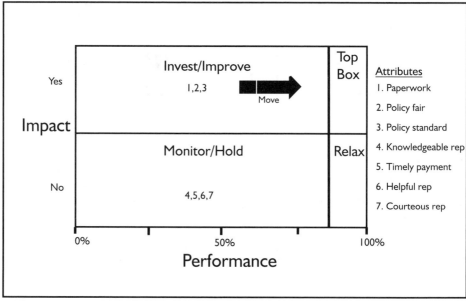

Figure 8–4. Decision matrix.

ably require some investment in either time and/or money. By contrast, those attributes that scored low and are considered unimportant to the servicer, that is, the lower left-hand box, should be monitored and all improvements put on hold.

FROM MANAGEMENT INFORMATION TO ACTION

As in so many customer situations, Jerry now must make some hard decisions from these soft numbers. In summary, here is what he did and why:

1. Being new in the job, Jerry thought it wise not to make too many improvements that would be major expense items.
2. From Figure 8–1, he could see that USA's performance on two major processes was significantly impacting servicer satisfaction.
3. Jerry also knew from past experience that dissatisfied servicers could well be mistreating USA customers and causing market damage. Jerry needed to select process improvements that were quick to implement, immediately recognizable to each servicer, and yet stay within a limited budget.
4. Jerry rationalized that potentially he should try to pick one item in each process to focus on for improvements, depending upon the cost—but how to choose which item?
5. Jerry first inspected Figure 8–2 to see what customers might be saying about the warranty claims process. Very obviously, the paperwork was getting terrible grades, and its impact was quite high. A cursory investigation of the claims paperwork by Jerry turned up the fact that the claims form was quite old, required redundant data already known to USA's accounting system, and that a new form using electronic mail would be easy and inexpensive to implement. In addition, Jerry set a goal for the claims department to reduce the paperwork complaints from an average of 122 per month to 50 per month or less.
6. Next, Jerry studied Figure 8–3, where parts availability seemed like the obvious choice. Unfortunately, further investigation showed that parts were in short supply nationally, although product was in ample supply. Manufacturing was forecasting that the parts availability problem would take 60 days to correct. The market damage

potential was so great with customers not being able to use their USA products that Jerry got approval for a product "loaner" program. With this program servicers could replace "in kind" equipment with a loaner to customers to keep them happy during the parts shortage. Jerry set a goal to reduce the parts shortage complaints from a whopping 348 per month to less than 25 per month.

7. Once Jerry had decided on all the changes, he wrote a very pleasant letter to all the USA service centers and told the managers about all the changes that had come about because of their valuable inputs from the survey. Jerry knew that he was laying the ground for an even more successful customer relationship survey the next time around. By telling the service center managers that he was making changes because of their inputs he was actually proving to them that USA listened to its customers and valued their suggestions and concerns.

LESSONS LEARNED

✔ An impact/performance bar chart can quickly and effectively show where actions are best taken by management to improve satisfaction.

✔ Frequently, changes indicated by analyzing customer surveys are not expensive to implement.

✔ Unhappy service center personnel can cause market damage to end-user customers.

✔ When you make a change based upon having surveyed customers (or in this case servicers), don't keep it a secret. Telling customers that you are making a change because of the results of a survey actually convinces them that you do listen, and these same customers will be even more willing to "sound off" the next time you ask them "How are we doing?" with a survey.

✔ A decision matrix can be helpful in obtaining management's attention to where to invest to bring performance in line with impact.

9

Changing Corporate Cultures

INTRODUCTION

In the preceding chapters, we have focused on qualitative and quantitative methods for managing customer relationships. These techniques all point to how to get the customer involved in the design and implementation of a company's processes.

FUZZY LOGIC 9.1

> *"Let the customer decide for you."*

Figure 9–1 summarizes what we have been discussing thus far. By monitoring the five basic SERVQUAL (Berry & Parasuraman, 1991) attributes that customers expect in each of your company's processes, you can continuously improve the customer-perceived value of your product, and thereby achieve long-term customer retention and loyalty.

FUZZY LOGIC 9.2

> *"Let the customer define the outcome of each of your company's processes."*

Customers do care what a company does to help them achieve their desired outcomes. By aligning business goals with the customer's purpose, companies can maintain viability in the rapidly changing environment of customer relationships.

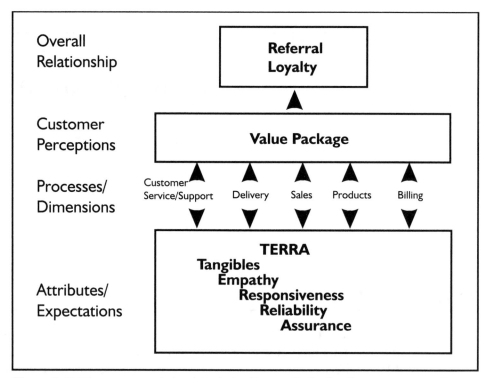

Figure 9–1. The customer relationship chain. (Source: K. Banks, Cummins Engine Co.)

Listening to the voice of the customer, and taking action based on the voice of the customer are two very different activities. Without a top-down mindset to include the customer in every decision, company managers quickly revert to inwardly focused decision making, which is basically a financial-only focus.

For example, given the sophistication of today's information technology systems, it's easy to check a computerized order entry system and spot which customers have defected. The real challenge is to find managers who will make use of that information to improve the service process, reduce defection levels, and strengthen the business.

A great customer relationship strategy is not enough. You need management commitment to customer satisfaction, plus empowered, motivated, and well-trained employees.

FUZZY LOGIC 9.3

"When the customer is invited to advise you on how to operate your business, you are rewarded by positive referrals and product loyalty."

If a customer service representative (CSR) is not able to make a person feel that his or her problem is the most important concern at the time, then what started as a small issue can turn into a problem that ends up costing you that customer.

A focus on customer relationships and satisfaction as the central point for organizational strategy and management philosophy requires a shift in corporate culture. The delivery of customer service and satisfaction means nothing if there is no management support structure to support a change in corporate culture. As demonstrated in Figure 9–2, when making changes to a process to better meet the needs of customers, you may find that the people working in the process are difficult, if not impossible, to change. Therefore, a change in process often requires a change to employees that are more customer-focused.

FUZZY LOGIC 9.4

"Service is the link between the producer and customers, both internal and external."

Too many of today's CEOs are managing companies that have marginal balance sheets, highly structured and internally organized departments with

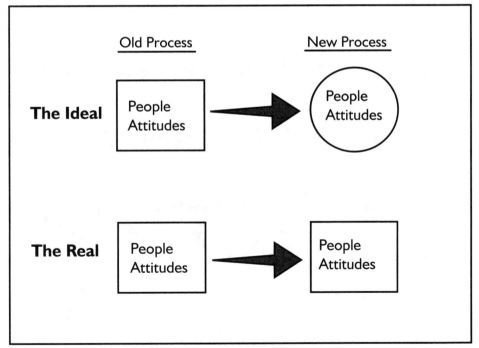

Figure 9–2. Different focus—different people.

undertrained and undermotivated employees, and a frightening lack of strength to change. These executives are inundated with an ever-increasing volume of financial data and worthless reports. And they are still using obsolete techniques that don't help solve the problem. As a result, too many companies are "frozen in the headlights" of customer-driven changes.

Current experience would suggest that traditional management structures cannot support the cultural and managerial changes needed to become truly customer-focused. In this chapter we will discuss some ways to facilitate a change in corporate culture toward the customer.

DEFINING CUSTOMER FOCUS

Customer focus is an arrangement of the company and its people that leads to predictably positive experiences for customers. As shown in Figure 9–3, this organizational focus comes about only through the development of a

Figure 9–3. Organizational focus.

corporate culture that keeps a constant eye on whether both the internal and external customer needs are being met or exceeded.

The objective of being customer focused is to provide an experience over time such that the customer will view the company as the supplier of choice. Easy to define, difficult to implement, or in other words, "easy to talk the talk," much more difficult to "walk the walk."

FUZZY LOGIC 9.5

> *"In today's business world, to retain customers you cannot look at it as if you were selling a product. Instead, you are providing customer-perceived value."*

COMPANY FOCUS DETERMINES OUTCOME

Today's losers are internally focused, functionally managed, and management-centered. The following columns compare and contrast the two corporate mindsets:

Profit-Focused	*Customer-Focused*
Standards are adhered to	Customer designs usability
Technical skills dominate	Interpersonal skills are key
Only salespersons deal directly with the customer	Everyone deals with and listens to the customer
Policies are difficult to change	Flexibility is encouraged
Financials are the focus	Fuzzy logic of customer relationships is the focus
Profitability is number one	Customer satisfaction is number one

For most companies that want to transition both structurally and culturally to become customer-focused, the re-engineering effort will require taking a careful look at their business processes and the technology that supports them. But instead of using computers to speed up existing work processes, companies must use information technology to achieve the larger business goals of improving customer relationships.

In today's markets, there exists a disparate need for business, large and small, to transform to a customer-focused approach. However, companies must avoid getting caught in the trap of using automation to perpetuate, and make more efficient, bad work processes.

CREATING A CUSTOMER-FOCUSED CULTURE

In our experience in assisting companies to create a customer-focused culture, we have found that the following are steps are worth considering:

1. Define all your business in terms of a continuous service to your customers, from pre-sales to post-sales activities. Change the emphasis from structure and systems to innovation, cross-functional thinking, and decentralized, strategic decision making. Flatten the organization and bring it closer to the customer. Think like a customer.

2. Identify and differentiate customers in terms of their roles, power, special characteristics, and needs. No business can expect to satisfy all customers, therefore target very specific products/services for very specific, niche, target customers. Bring new people into the organization to inject fresh thinking and to be catalysts in the drive to change. We are aware of several large banks that are implementing customer information systems that allow them to "customerize" their products for specific target customers. For instance, some of these banks provide PC banking to consumers and businesses alike to encourage self-help banking transactions.

3. Determine customers' prioritized expectations related to service product attributes (performance and perception) and outcome. For instance, Ford Motors talks of being a "transportation provider." Ford sees its business as cars, motorcycles, traffic management systems, and auto recycling. Whirlpool executives redefined their company's mission as a fabric-care or a food-preservation enterprise rather than a washing-machine or refrigerator manufacturer. Put in a holistic process for implementing change, a new method of working, that transcends the barriers, the "old baggage," and the mistrust and fear of change.

4. Continuously measure the degree to which expectations are met (perceived value). Manage the customers' experiences by actively soliciting feedback and acting on it promptly. Identify the costs and the output of every process, and then measure the impact of this on customer value, employee value, and shareholder value.

5. Maintain a current description of the service creation and delivery process with charts, text, and measures. Continually train, educate, and develop people as a strategic priority. Customer-satisfying service makes money, and it also saves money. Keeping customers reduces

marketing expenses, since not as many new customers are needed. Money unexpended on marketing equals profits retained. Foster curiosity and constant desire to improve among employees, an objective that's well within reach of all companies. The reputation of a company rides not only on the talents of management but equally on the communication skills of the employees. The customer's perception of the company's staff is the public image of the entire company. The Forum Corporation found that the factor most strongly related to employees retention was simply whether employees thought the organization was providing good service to its customers (Davis, 1992).

6. Establish and maintain internal and external metrics, to manage the customer relationships. For instance, in a call center, you would track blocked calls and time in queue; in an order entry department you might track incorrect invoices, and so on. The traditional productivity measure (output per labor-hour) is fine for wheat and steel, but is not adequate for the information age. Missing from those calculations is the role relationship management plays in improving customer service, inventory management, financial analysis, and other business functions.

To realign strategic business directions with the capabilities of new technology, a company must evaluate its existing architecture and retool the infrastructure to take advantage of low-cost and flexible hardware and software components using open, vendor-independent, standard interfaces. But more important than the retooling are the functional and cultural changes that must be made to the organization—these depend on management's openness to change and its determination to reorganize.

FOCUSING ON CUSTOMER RELATIONSHIP RECOVERY

Every complaint the average business receives represents about 2,000 unvoiced complaints about the same issue (Plymire, 1991). The American Management Association estimates that the average company may lose as many as 35 percent of its customers every year, adding up to several million dollars of lost revenue.

At any one time 27 percent of your customers are dissatisfied enough with your service to stop doing business with you—yet only 4 percent complain (Lawton, 1991). Ironically, the problems of noncomplainants are usually relatively easy to solve. If given a chance, companies could retain many of their dissatisfied customers.

Because of existing corporate cultures, most employees rarely encourage feedback. Why? Many have trouble hearing a complaint as feedback, instead they hear it as a personal attack on their self-esteem or their company. Training and cultural change are issues, and so is having the technology to track and manage customer complaints.

The following is a six-part process to encourage a corporate cultural change about complaints:

1. Train employees to view complaints as opportunities. Complaints are just another way of doing things, not good or bad, right or wrong.
2. Challenge employees about how many customer complaints they can document in one week.
3. The customers will start talking when they hear a willingness to listen. Instead of "How was your stay?" we might ask, "What one thing could we have done to improve your stay?" Instead of "How was your dinner?" we might ask, "What one thing could we do to improve your meal?"
4. Encourage employees to write down customer issues. This is valuable information. Some people will say that talking with customers may interfere with business.

FUZZY LOGIC 9.6

"Let's not forget that the customer is the only reason for our business."

5. Reward both complaint gatherers and complainers.
6. Emphasizing complaints as feedback will tell employees this is a customer-focused culture.

With the cost of keeping a customer only 20 percent of the cost of getting a new one, the smartest business move you could make is to spend money evaluating and improving your customer relationships.

Complaints and complaint management can be the key to future sales. If reducing complaints is a shortcut to oblivion, increasing complaints is the road to stardom. Every complaint is actually a very valuable piece of business intelligence.

CUSTOMER FOCUS: SATISFACTION/ RETENTION/PROFITS

Carefully designed investments in motivated people, equipped with information technology, will produce greater returns than similar investments in advertising/marketing. Companies like Motorola that have invested heavily in training and groupware, have documented savings of 30 times the dollars invested (Tanaka, 1991). According to one IBM executive, "If we can improve customer satisfaction by one percent, it means $257 million in revenue to us over the next five years."

In Figure 9–4 we show the chain of events emanating from a customer-focused organization. By focusing on more than just profits, this figure shows how all the pieces of the puzzle are related and connected. A properly designed customer-focused strategy feeds on its own success. Companies can boost profits 100 percent by retaining just 5 percent of their customers (Hughes, 1992).

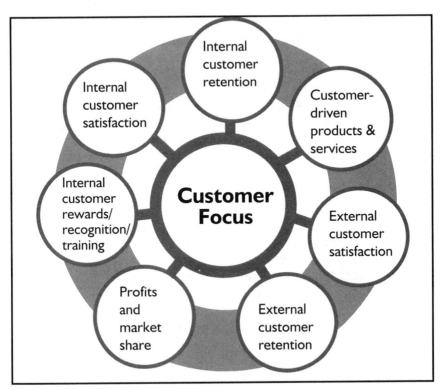

Figure 9–4. Why focus on customer satisfaction?

ORGANIZATIONAL STRUCTURE AND FORM NEEDED

There are four essential structural forms and two process that support customer-focused corporate cultures. These structures exist independently of each other but must be present in some form in order for any satisfaction efforts to succeed.

1. **Executive mission steering group.** One of the major problems facing a shift to a customer-focused organization is in shifting the top-level executives. All corporate cultural changes must reflect a high-level push and commitment for the change. The executive mission steering group is a high-level executive committee formed of top-level, highly respected executives. A top-level steering group gives coordination and direction and impetus to customer relationship improvement initiatives.

2. **Satisfaction support department.** Once customer-focus initiatives begin, there is generally no department whose mission is to support those efforts. Usually, the support functions go to employees who have no ownership and who see the work as simply more work in addition to their regular functions. A departmental function whose function is customer relationship management is required. The purpose of this group is to work through and remove internal obstacles to continuous improvement, and to provide the needed tools to get the job done quickly and efficiently.

3. **Strategic Wish Alternative Tactics (SWAT) teams.** The SWAT team is a cross-functional group of highly motivated and empowered employees who go to where the customer dissatisfaction problem surfaces, and focus on both a short-term customer recovery, and long-term strategy changes to avoid the problem in the future. They are quick and flexible, and have the authority to "get it done, whatever it takes." In our experience, most efforts to change companies require the short-term assignment of a SWAT team to lead specific change initiatives. Small is beautiful—and functional. These select groups of highly rewarded employees are brought together in a temporary assignment to analyze specific issues and make things happen for the customer.

4. **Information technology enablement.** It is often painfully clear to us that information technology within an organization can either

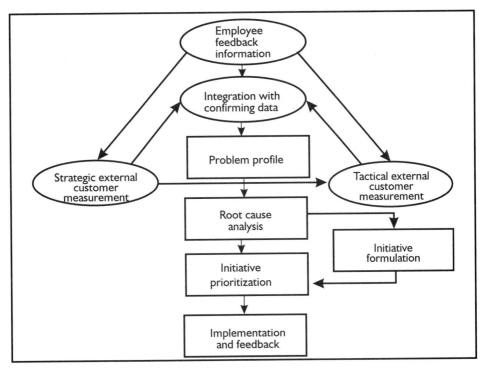

Figure 9–5. Customer-focused information system.

help or hinder the corporate culture change process. In Figure 9–5, we have outlined a customer relationship monitoring system design that can enable a company to become more customer-focused. By combining customer feedback and employee feedback along with a customer recovery process, management can have its finger on the pulse of the customer at all times. These customer information reports must become an integral part of the corporate culture to ensure quick and effective response to the ever-changing world of customer requirements.

LESSONS LEARNED

✔ Don't underestimate normal people's resistance to change.

✔ Corporate culture changes begin by total commitment from the top.

✔ New customer-focused processes managed by old internally focused employees result in a return to being internally focused.

✔ Employees thrive on working for companies with satisfied customers.

✔ Information technology can enable corporate culture changes.

10

Case Studies

INTRODUCTION

In order to further convince the reader that it is possible to quantitatively and qualitatively listen to the voice of the customer, we have summarized five actual business cases where customer relationship information was gathered, analyzed, and interpreted to improve management decision-making ability.

Although the cases discussed in this chapter are real, we have changed the names of the companies and the individuals working there to protect their anonymity.

CASE 1 *To Go Beyond Patient Satisfaction*

Case Overview

In a new atmosphere of competition, characterized increasingly by private initiative, health-care providers are realizing that they should become more customer-focused for a number of important reasons, namely:

1. Reduced insurance benefits and increases in co-payments and deductibles are becoming more widespread. As a result, patients are more sensitive to getting their money's worth—value—and less likely to use health services indiscriminately.
2. Patients perceive their time to be valuable and they are unwilling to waste it in hospital waiting rooms. The passive role of patients is being replaced

with an active demand for personalized, attentive, and courteous service at a reasonable price.

3. With ample competitors eager for their patronage, patients no longer have to be satisfied with substandard care; they can shop for health-care services or may decide to switch from one service provider to another. Alternatively, patients that are satisfied, or delighted, are more apt to use the health service again in the future.

The Board of Directors of the Park Ridge Health Maintenance Organization (PRHMO) is very much aware of this need to become customer focused. PRHMO consists of three ambulatory health centers. In addition to the clinic department for treatment of illnesses, the PRHMO centers also offer a wide range of preventive health-care services such as medical checkups and programs for smoking cessation, nutrition and diet counseling. PRHMO's strategic plan for the nineties, "Customer Care 2000," breathes customer satisfaction. Patient satisfaction is measured continually by using comment cards containing the items shown in Table 10–1.1.

While the satisfaction index numbers in Table 10–1.1 are used to reveal trends in patients' perceptions, they remain abstract and hardly suggest any concrete areas where the service should be improved. And there is a drastic need for improvement, as the downward trends in Table 10–1.1 show.

At the same time the Board realizes that mere patient satisfaction might no longer be enough in the near future. Already it has become clear that *customer delight* (providing "wow-experiences") will be a decisive weapon in the competitive health services battlefield. The Board also realizes that the flip side of patient delight is *patient discontent,* that is, dissatisfaction to such a degree that patients simply will terminate their relationship with PRHMO and switch to a

TABLE 10–1.1. **PRHMO's Satisfaction Measurement System**

Question	1st quarter 1994	1st quarter 1993
Overall satisfaction	5.4	5.3
Doctor communication	6.1*	6.5
Doctor attitude	5.7*	6.4
Doctor willingness to spend time	5.3*	5.8
Support staff attitude	4.6	4.9
Waiting time lobby	4.8	4.7
Waiting time exam room	5.4	5.3

* = Statistically significant

competitor. Customer discontent clearly falls outside the so-called zones of tolerance. Figure 10–1.1 indicates the "service performance space" in which PRHMO has to maneuver and which areas it has to avoid.

The Vice President of Operations, Nancy McDowell, as been given the task of exploring this service performance space and determining where the critical boundaries lie. She has to come up with actionable information for service improvements and the planning of new patient services that lead to patient delight. She decides to let the patients define delight and discontent, using the critical incident technique (CIT).

The Critical Incident Technique

As discussed in Chapter 3, the CIT invites customers to come up with actual examples of exceptionally good and bad service. In this way very detailed information can be obtained on the aspects that make customers tick. This method also yields a number of illustrative instances that can be used for personnel training and new service development. In the PRHMO case respondents were invited to describe

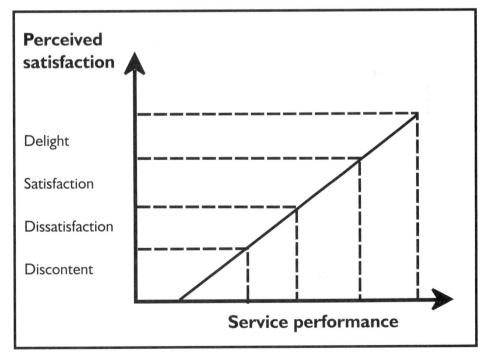

Figure 10–1.1. The service performance space.

a specific interaction between patients and PRHMO employees and specific observations that were perceived to be especially satisfying or especially dissatisfying.

The critical incidents had to meet the following criteria: They had to (1) be specific, (2) relate to a distinct visit to a PRH clinic; (3) describe the respondent's perception in terms of distinctive adjectives, and (4) incidents had to refer specifically to an aspect of service. In addition to the central incident-based question, a number of closed-ended questions were added for quantitative analysis. Finally, patients were asked to indicate the effect of each specific incident on their patronage behavior.

Data Collection

Nancy McDowell had two professional interviewers do the data collection. Here are some statistics. In total, 221 mini-interviews were held with a randomly selected sample of patients of health maintenance organizations (HMOs). According to PRHMO's clinical records, the interviewees represented a cross section of its own customer base. Sixty-three percent of the respondents were female, and 37 percent of the respondents were males. Other interviewee demographics included age, specialist seen, frequency of visit, and means of transportation to the clinic.

Fifty-two percent of the respondents were less than 50 years old. Fifty-seven percent of the respondents visited the clinic at least four times during the last twelve months. Thirty-two percent of the respondents came to see a diet consultant. Other specialists that were frequently visited were general surgeons (19%), eye surgeons (11%), and gynecologists (7%). The majority (73%) of the respondents used a car as their means of transportation to visit the clinic. Of the critical incidents 43 (12%) failed to meet at least one of the criteria discussed previously, leaving a total sample of 481 usable incidents. One hundred and ninety respondents could mention at least one positive incident, while 113 (51%) could mention two positive incidents. One hundred and forty-four respondents brought forward at least one negative incident, while 47 (21%) reported two negative incidents. Within the sample, 8.6 % of the customers could mention as many as four negative incidents.

Data Analysis

The incidents were analyzed through a three-step classification method. In the first place, they were classified into 128 codes on the basis of their content. These codes then organized into 30 subcategories. Subsequently, the subcategories were classified into five categories: "tangibles" (e.g., interior design, signs), "reliability" (e.g., competent staff, waiting time), "responsiveness" (e.g., waiting list, willingness to provide information), "assurance" (e.g., quality of information provided) and "empathy" (e.g., personal approach, privacy). Classification of incidents was done independently by two researchers from a local college. The two data coders agreed on about 75 percent of the incidents the first time. For classification of the remaining incidents a consensus was reached between both researchers in a meeting with Nancy McDowell.

Table 10–1.2 gives the distribution of the critical incidents at the category level.

From Data to Management Information

From the data it could be concluded that the health service environment is the major source of discontent—57 percent of the negative critical incidents relate to the category "tangibles." Alternatively, the category "empathy" seems to be the primary source for delight: 46 percent of the positive critical incidents can be viewed as factors leading to a wow experience. The two prevailing sources of patient delight and discontent are broken down into subcategories in Figures 10–1.2 and 10–1.3. In addition, Table 10–1.3 offers samples of the incidents that were collected at subcategory level for the dimensions "tangibles" and "empathy." In addition, respondents were asked to indicate what the effect of the critical incident was on their relationship with the particular HMO. Table 10–1.4 indicates the distribution across the multiple options.

It can be concluded that patient discontent has a profound effect on the patient-clinic relationship and that switching barriers are low. It appeared from the interviews that an important reason behind why some patients' relationships were actually strengthened was the fact that these discontented patients complained, and immediately received a "delighting" response to their complaint.

TABLE 10–1.2. **Distribution Critical Incidents at Major Category Level**

	Positive		Negative		Total	
Incidents	*n*	*%*	*n*	*%*	*n*	*%*
Tangibles	51	17.53	109	57.36	161	33.25
Reliability	49	16.84	41	21.58	90	18.71
Responsiveness	43	14.78	20	10.53	63	13.10
Assurance	15	5.15	6	3.16	21	4.37
Empathy	133	45.70	14	7.37	147	30.56
Total	291	100.00	190	100.00	481	100.00

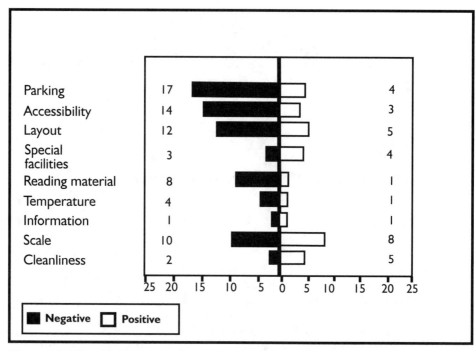

Figure 10–1.2. Incidents at subcategory level "tangibles."

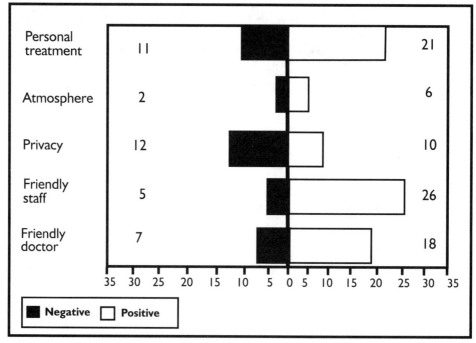

Figure 10–1.3. Incidents at subcategory level "empathy."

TABLE 10–1.3. **Sample Incidents**

Subcategory	Type	Sample incident
101. Car parking	–	When I wanted to park my car at a disabled space there wasn't any room. Whenever two out of the three disabled spaces are taken, you can't use the third.
102. Convenience of location	–	My wheelchair could not be pushed up the slope in front of the main entrance by my husband. It was too steep, it took too much effort.
105. Special facilities	–	When I had to be taken to the first aid room of this clinic I had to lay down on a stretcher with a very thin sort of canvas. Because I suffer from rheumatism this was a very painful experience to me.
106. Reading material	–	Last week I noticed that the reading materials in the waiting room were from 1988. The only recent magazines were medical magazines. These are not very interesting.
107. Temperature	–	When I was in the waiting room in the old part of the clinic I nearly caught a cold. There was a terrible draft because the doors no longer close properly.
501. Personal approach	+	During my last visit the doctor's secretary remembered my name and asked me how things were at home.
503. Reception	+	When I brought my child the doctor made a special effort to make her feel at ease. They are good with children.
504. Privacy	–	The doctor left the door of the room ajar. Everybody could overhear us.
506. Attitude, doctors	+	The doctor who is very friendly promised to sing me a song and bring cakes as the next appointment had to be scheduled on my birthday.

TABLE 10–1.4. **The Effect of Patient Discontent on Patient Patronage Behavior**

Options Open to Discontented Patients	*%*
"I never went back" (Relationship broken)	48
"I went back less frequently" (Relationship weakened)	24
"I went back as often as ever" (Relationship unchanged)	12
"I went back more frequently" (Relationship strengthened)	26

From Management Information to Action

The results suggested a number of ways in which sources for patient discontent could be eliminated. Some of these follow directly followed from the incidents, were straightforward, and required little investment by PRHMO management—for example, (1) updating of waiting room reading materials, (2) extending the disabled parking space, and (3) adapting doors of elevators for the disabled. Other service improvements will require more consideration (e.g., the purchase of specialized new equipment) and will be discussed during the next round of budgeting.

While it is often relatively easy to make changes in the tangible department, it is much harder to influence the attitude and behavior of employees. However, the specificity of the results obtained by means of the CIT makes them particularly applicable for personnel training. Two training programs were designed for the purpose of developing current and future employee communication and empathy skills. In testing these programs, the use of concrete examples and hands-on knowledge in training could be used to enhance the ability of personnel to observe, identify and study personnel behavior in the context of patient discontent.

In the area of customer delight a considerable investment was made in the development a patient information database for employee to use when in contact with a patient. This on-line information gives the employee access to a record containing personalized information (last visit, birthdays, etc.). In this way, a level of personalization could be obtained and WOW experiences could be planned ahead in service encounters. Finally, on the basis of the CIT study, a new monthly patient survey was designed for continuous monitoring of patient delight and discontent.

LESSONS LEARNED

✔ The CIT enables organizations to obtain a truly customer-defined picture of the quality of their service.

✔ The CIT identifies those factors that define what "knock-your-socks-off" service is all about.

✔ The CIT provides hands-on knowledge of what really happens in the service encounter resulting in very concrete service improvement suggestions.

✔ The CIT combines the power of numbers with the depth of interviews, that is, the quantitative with the qualitative

✔ Hard decisions can be made with soft numbers.

CASE 2   *The Calculus of Customer Relationships*

Case Overview

One might say that Hans Vandenberg, Senior Vice President of Customer Relations at the European headquarters of Waxx, a world-leading apparel manufacturer, has his act together. His 24-hour-a-day operation, a state-of-the-art call center located in Amsterdam, is frequently visited by benchmarkers from many different industries. The customer relations call center handles inbound calls from all European countries where Waxx products are marketed, including the recently explored markets of Poland and Hungary. In the center, 78 native-speaking representatives are employed dealing with nearly 200,000 customer- and retailer-initiated communications that are routed to Amsterdam every year. A toll-free number is posted in retail stores and in Waxx advertising. In addition, Waxx proactively approaches consumers and retail partners for feedback. Several customer and retail surveys are fielded and processed in all European countries by the center. The customer relations center uses advanced information technology to process this enormous amount of customer data.

The large majority of the inbound calls from both customers and retailers (67%) relate to requests for information. To deal with these requests, Hans has designed an extensive where-to-buy database that has an on-line connection to the six major Waxx distribution centers in Europe. Moreover, information on shipments from East Asia, where Waxx's major production facilities are located, is downloaded every night to ensure that up-to-date information can be given to callers.

The most important advantages for such a strong centralization of customer relationship management are:

1. Control and consistency of information collection, processing, and warehousing
2. High accessibility of information for knowledge workers
3. Staff availability and professionalism

In the Waxx Management Report, which is a monthly update of important management information, the center has been awarded two pages in which trends in customer relationships are reported. So, in terms of the information infrastructure, Hans's center is considered very successful.

However, there is also a very important disadvantage to the company's centralized approach to customer relationship management. This is primarily related to the 28 percent of the inbound calls that are complaints from consumers and retailers. While these have been labelled as top priority by management, the actual followup to complaints falls under the responsibility of the General Sales Manager (GSM) in each country. Unfortunately, a general picture that keeps recurring is one of considerable delay in the handling of these complaints. Too often complaints are simply lost in the web of the national sales organizations. The GSMs have been paying lip service rather than real service to detecting causes of consumer dissatisfaction. This is not new to Hans. For years he has been trying to advance consumer complaints on the priority list of the GSMs. He has been feeding them satisfaction indices, he has shown the negative effect on the Waxx brand image, he even had the company president address the issue in a personalized letter.

Yet, a downward trend in customer satisfaction with complaint handling keeps emerging from both consumer and retailer surveys. Time and time again the center's information is greeted with skepticism. Hans realizes that the GSMs primarily think in terms of Deutsche marks, lire, francs, pesetas—money. Therefore, he decided to address them in a language they understand. He will no longer wait to be invited to the party so he organizes his own. When the GSMs are flown into Amsterdam for the annual sales meeting, Hans invites all of them to participate in an early afternoon, one-hour seminar. During the seminar he demonstrates his method for calculating the value of customer relationships with the aim of turning the skeptic GSMs into change artists instead. Hans wants them to take ownership of customer complaints.

Customer Relationship Measurement

Hans views customer complaints as an opportunity to restore satisfaction. If complaints are opportunities, then ineffective handling will present lost opportunity costs. The calculus of the customer relationship method keeps track of the lost opportunity costs of each broken-off relationship. It combines customer data with financial data. It also takes into account the market damage of negative word-of-mouth. The calculus makes customer relationships come alive in money terms.

The method consists of a three-step process:

1. A theoretical sample of 100 dissatisfied customers is taken to illustrate the calculations. This step serves to let management buy into the method. After a detailed analysis, a theoretical lost customer ratio is presented and the seeds for support are planted.
2. A practical example based on actual company data is taken to calculate the lost opportunity costs of broken-off relationships. Again, after the calculations, the lost customer ratio is presented this time in terms of the actual amounts, and the persuasion factor is multiplied.
3. Then, for maximum impact, the longer-term value of a customer relationship is calculated over several intervals of time.

The method's main purpose is to motivate company management to pay attention to the consequences of customer dissatisfaction. Too often comments like "I hardly ever meet a dissatisfied customer" or "Eight complaints out of 75,000 products shipped last month—big deal!" can be heard.

In presenting the calculations, Hans gives his audience a blank sheet and requests them to participate in the calculations (of course, he has the actual numbers ready to serve as backup). In order to visualize the calculations, he simply keeps a tally (by drawing unhappy faces) so that his audience can easily follow him. Hans knows from experience that management often underestimates the opportunity costs of poor service. As a result, the value of a customer relationship is calculated with statistics that are too optimistic. He also knows that he never fails to astonish and impress his audience.

Data Collection

In order to perform the calculus of customer relationships two basic types of data are needed—customer data and financial data. The customer data can be obtained from customer-initiated communications, such as complaints from periodic or continual customer surveys. Specifically the following data types are required:

- The number of dissatisfied customers
- The number of dissatisfied customers who complain
- The number of dissatisfied customers who complain and do not repurchase the company's products
- The number of dissatisfied customers who do not complain and do not repurchase
- The number of customers who are subjected to negative word-of-mouth by complaining customers
- The number of customers who do not purchase due to negative word-of-mouth
- The number of customers who are subjected to negative word-of-mouth by noncomplaining customers
- The number of customers who do not purchase due to negative word-of-mouth by noncomplaining customers

In addition, the following internal financial data types are needed:

- The average buying frequency of the most important consumer target groups
- The average profit of the most important products
- The average annual price increase

These numbers were collected by Hans for his mini-seminar. Here's how he used them in a three-step analysis of the financial value of customer relationships.

Data Analysis

In his presentation to the GSM Hans starts with 100 unhappy WAXX customers in what he calls a warming up example. The results of step 1 are shown Figure 10–2.1.

First he asks them how many unhappy customers they think will complain directly to the Waxx Customer Relations Center. Several numbers are brought forward by the audience and a consensus is reached at four customers out of 100 would actually complain. This means that 96 will not voice their dissatisfaction. Of those customers that do complain, it is estimated that only 10 percent will not repurchase Waxx products again. Theoretically, this means that .4 of the complaining customers will break off their relationship with Waxx. This 10 percent that does not repurchase anymore will generate negative word-of-mouth by telling 5 other people on average. Of all the people that are told the negative stories about Waxx only 2 percent will not repurchase. So far, this gives us the effect of dissatisfaction on the segment of Waxx customers that take the trouble to complain.

Next, in step 2, we must conclude that there are 96 percent unhappy consumers that simply say "hasta la vista." Of this segment, the GSMs pose that approximately 30 percent will not repurchase again due to Waxx's strong brand loyalty. Hans explains that the data from Waxx customer surveys suggests a far more higher percentage (78%), but he decides to play along and use the optimistic statistic brought forward by his audience. The 30 percent that break off their relationship with Waxx will tell nine other consumers about their negative experience, according to the GSMs. Finally, the GSMs agree that of all the people that are confronted with negative word-of-mouth, 2 percent also will not repurchase Waxx products again. Hans assures his audience that this is certainly not a worst-case scenario.

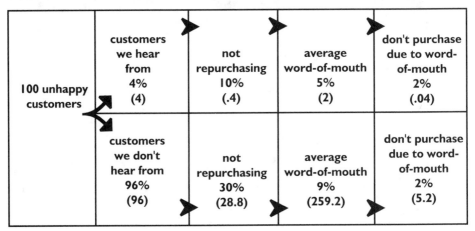

Figure 10–2.1. A warming-up example.

Adding up customers lost directly and indirectly through negative word of mouth, the lost customer ratio is .34. This means that out of every 100 unhappy customers Waxx loses 34. This is subsequently extrapolated on the basis of actual Waxx data, as shown in Figure 10–2.2.

Now, the statistics really come alive, as they reflect the actual Waxx situation. Hans simply starts filling in the numbers. On the basis of the Waxx customer survey system, it is known that 164,475 consumers from all over Europe experienced problems related to Waxx products between August 1993 and August 1994. Of those unhappy consumers, 6,579 voiced their dissatisfaction to the customer relations call center via the toll-free number. If 10 percent of those consumers do not intend to repurchase, Waxx loses 658 customers. Due to the fact that the negative word spreads easily they lose an additional 66. The large majority of the unhappy consumers (157,896) do not bother to let Waxx know. Of these 96 percent of the total number of unhappy customers— 47,369—will no longer use Waxx products in the future. As a result of negative word-of-mouth another 8,526 customers will be lost. The conclusion is that Waxx has lost 56,619 consumers due to dissatisfaction in one year. Again, Hans assures his audience that these are very conservative estimates.

From Data to Management Information

In step 3 of the calculus of customer relationships, the long-term value of a customer's relationship is calculated over several intervals of time. Waxx caters to relatively young market segments as studies from the market research department have shown. For the sake of simplicity and argument, Hans asks his audience to think of two basic segments and to assume that the number of unhappy customers can be equally divided among those segments. This means

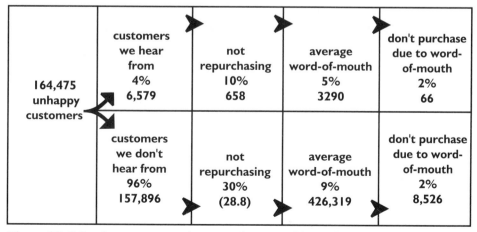

Figure 10–2.2. Lost customers between August, 1993 and August, 1994.

that 28,310 of the unhappy are less than 30 years old, and that 28,310 are over 30 years old. Furthermore, according to WAXX market research data, the average customer under 30 will buy 93.8 jeans and 51.1 slacks in the rest of his or her life, while the older category will on average buy 58.4 jeans and 36.1 slacks.

The company's financial data show that the profit margin for a pair of jeans is 16.50 ECU (the common European currency), while for slacks the profit margin is 17.75 ECU. At a 3 percent price increase this means that the lifetime value of the average person under 30 is 5,724 ECU and the lifetime value of an average person over 30 is 3,008 ECU. Hans asks his audience whether they are still with him before putting on his last sheet on which the numbers for the past year are extrapolated over longer time periods. He reminds them once again that the estimates that formed the basis for the exercise where suggested by the members of the audience, and that these numbers are not an accurate representation of the real situation. His last sheet is shown in Figure 10–2.3.

From Management Information to Action

The GSMs are impressed. In the discussion following the presentation of the calculus of customer relationships, the formation of a SWAT team is suggested by several members of the audience to improve root cause analysis of dissatisfaction within the national Waxx sales organizations. Over the period of one year, the committee consisting of three GSMs and Hans acting as a secretary will spend fifteen person days:

- Establishing complaint followup goals
- Linking goals to reward and recognition programs
- Modifying/enhancing policies and procedures
- Formulating accountability
- Improving support systems and facilities
- Redesigning report formats
- Targeting specific future priorities
- Identifying best practices

It was agreed that in cooperation with each country the calculus of customer relationships will be carried out and presented at the 1995 GSM meet-

1 Year	5 Years	10 Years	Lifetime
3.206.327 ECU	16.493.927 ECU	34.875.528 ECU	247.257.171 ECU

Figure 10–2.3. The calculus of customer relationships.

ing. Also, it was collectively agreed that each GSM would undergo a "tour of duty" by spending a full day at the frontline of customer service in the customer relation call center.

LESSONS LEARNED

✔ The calculus of customer relationships is very convincing for obtaining management's buy-in to improvement efforts by addressing them in their own language (money), and allowing them to provide the assumptions.

✔ The calculus of customer relationships can lead to a company-wide initiative and avoids "pigeonholing" customer relationship to just one department.

✔ The calculus of customer relationships is a practical and simple way of pinpointing the lost opportunity costs of poor service.

✔ The calculus of customer relationships emphasizes the need for integrating and combining customer data with in-company financial data.

CASE 3 *Introducing the Teletary*

Case Overview

Associated Computer Engineers (ACE) is a large manufacturer of computer hardware and related accessories. While the company's name might suggest otherwise, ACE is a marketing-driven company. For example, by closely following marketplace trends, the company was able to survive the recent dip in the computer industry. Recently, marketing activities have become complex and diversified as the number of resellers has increased and because the company has (successfully) entered the home-computer market. At the same time, the company has moved from downsizing to rightsizing. The ACE marketing workforce has been on the move a lot. Many of the 9,000 representatives have moved between offices in the four operating regions. Moreover, most marketing representatives spend their time either on the road or at customer sites.

Despite these movements, the administrative structure of the marketing organization has remained unchanged during the last decade. This is probably the main reason behind a considerable increase in customer complaints as received by the company's call center. The most frequent complaints revolve around the lack of accessibility and responsiveness of the various teams within the marketing organization. And since customer relationships are maintained primarily through the telephone (86 percent of customer contacts take place over the phone), the marketing management team had expressed a serious concern when confronted with this increase in consumer complaints. In fact, there were already a number of customers who had second-sourced ACE by taking their new business elsewhere, and some clients had cancelled their service contracts as they simply could not get in touch with their ACE contact person.

At the same time, within the company frustration was gradually building up. ACE marketing executives were finding it very difficult to talk to their staff while on the road. Furthermore, the majority of the company's secretaries were complaining that they were spending 75 percent of their time answering phone calls and that they had no time left for doing other value-added tasks. In order to diagnose accessibility and responsiveness accurately and to determine service quality standards, the marketing management team outsourced a baseline study to a consulting firm specializing in this area of relationship problem solving. The firm proposed doing a telephone efficiency audit, making use of the mystery caller method (MCM) to investigate and document the problem of ACE's lack of accessibility and responsiveness to customers.

The Mystery Caller Method

The MCM is a simple but efficient way of measuring the telephone service quality in a systematic manner. During a given time period calls are made to a company (and to individual employees) on the basis of various scenarios. During the mystery calls, a number of features are registered. These include quantitative measures such as accessibility and response time and qualitative measures such as friendliness, professionalism, and so on. Ease of access to a company is measured by observing the following:

1. Customer awareness of the number to call to get the desired service
2. The ability to get through on the first call
3. The availability of the right service professional when needed
4. Being assisted by the first person reached

Customer accessibility can be measured on three different levels:

1. The call-center for which a toll-free number is used
2. The company's central telephone number, often located at reception
3. The individual teams or departments within a company (i.e., direct dials).

Response time can be defined in terms of the number of rings or in actual seconds. The time on hold is also included in response time calculations.

Data Collection

During nine weeks the consulting firm's telephone representatives made 7,452 mystery calls to the company. These included calls to the company's call center, the receptionist, and individual company employees of the various marketing teams. Names, phone numbers, and job descriptions were provided by ACE. Calls included requests for product and where-to-buy information, complaints, and specific questions addressed to ACE employees. It was announced in the company newsletter that the audit would take place but not when. In order to obtain a reliable picture of ACE's customer service on the phone, part of the holiday season was also included in the audit.

Data Analysis

Response time as well as accessibility were calculated with the help of a computer program. The following qualitative aspects were measured on a scale of 1 to 5: politeness, empathy, friendliness, professionalism, helpfulness, and audibility. In order to achieve intercoder reliability, 10 percent of the calls were taped and rated by other reps. Due to the professionalism and experience of these reps a high intercoder reliability of 92 percent could be obtained.

From Data to Management Information

The results of the ACE audit were compared to the computer industry standards available from the consulting firm. This is shown in Figures 10–3.1 and 10–3.2.

It is clear that the ACE toll-free and central numbers compare well in terms of accessibility and response time. On the other hand, there is a significant difference in the case of the marketing teams. Also, in qualitative terms the overall quality of ACE telephone communication remains largely below the industry norm as becomes painfully clear from Figure 10–3.3. This confirms the early-warning signals sent by unhappy ACE customers.

From Management Information to Action

From the MCM baseline study it can clearly be concluded that there is room for improvement of the telephone service quality of the ACE marketing organization. The ACE marketing management team decided not to opt for a technical solution to the problem; previous research had shown that the majority of

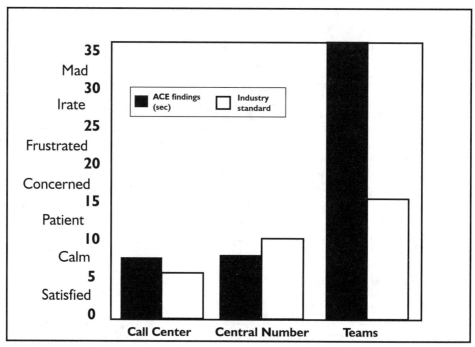

Figure 10–3.1.   Response time scores.

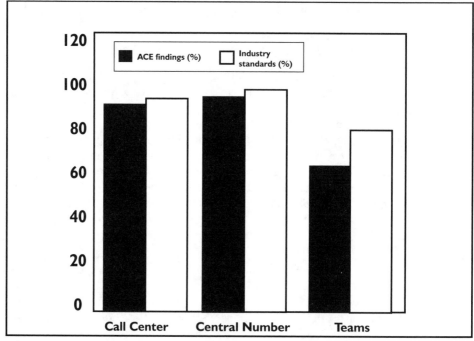

Figure 10–3.2.   Accessibility.

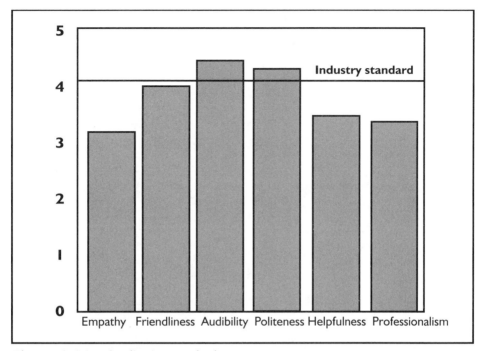

Figure 10–3.3. Qualitative standards.

ACE relations did not like the use of voice response technology. Instead, structural and staffing solutions were implemented.

A teletary support center was created at each of the four regional offices. The staff of these centers, called "teletaries," form a central point of contact for calls directed at the various teams that are left unanswered. All direct dial calls are routed via a teletary if they are not answered within three rings. Teletaries can take messages, make appointments, and provide information. In this way they take over an important part of the workload of departmental secretaries. The teletaries manage the electronic diary of every ACE marketing representative.

Of course, it was clear at the outset that updating diaries would be a make-or-break factor. For this reason an employee reward and recognition program was introduced. The basic principles of this system are shown in Table 10–3.1.

As a follow-up to the baseline study, the market research department will be monitoring regional marketing's performance each month, making use of the MCM. In this way each team can score in terms of accessibility and responsiveness. Points can be cashed in by trading them for social activities within the department. The scores of the various teams are published bimonthly with the help of the *Response Thermometer* in the company newsletter.

Other ways of embedding accessibility and responsiveness in personnel behavior include a number of short training sessions, presentations of the MCM

TABLE 10–3.1. The ACE Accessibility Bonus System

The AA Bonus System	
Accessibility:	
> 80%	2 points
75–80%	1 point
70–74%	0 points
60–69%	−1 point
< 60%	−2 points
Response Time:	
< 4 sec	3 points
4–5 sec	2 points
6–7 sec	1 point
8–10 sec	0 points
11–12 sec	−1 points
> 13 sec	−2 points

baseline study to the various teams, and a personalized letter sent to every employee's home address on the importance of providing quality customer service over the phone. Moreover, a small booklet called *A Toolbox for Providing Customer-Focused Telephone Service* was made available to every ACE marketing representative. In the booklet issues such as the tele-business card, telephone guidelines, and spelling are addressed.

LESSONS
LEARNED

✔ The MCM provides a detailed insight in how customer relationship management can be improved in terms of telephone efficiency and effectiveness.

✔ The MCM is a management-by-numbers approach to telephone service quality.

✔ The MCM is reasonably inexpensive and simple to apply.

✔ The MCM can provide a number of telephone transcripts illustrative of how to maintain and how not to maintain customer relationships.

CASE 4 *Profiling the Customer Value*

Case Overview

Douglas K. Saunders has recently been appointed as Chief Operating Officer (COO) for The Ambassador Suites Group, a national hotel chain. Having worked as a hotel manager for six years at Holiday Inn, he established his reputation as a goal-achieving-manager in the hotel business. Although Ambassador Suites has a quality image and a solid loyal guest base, almost unnoticeably, its market share had declined for the first time in twelve years in 1993. So, Doug made it his goal to strengthen guest relationships with Ambassador Suites.

Looking for clues, he began reviewing the guest comment card system, which had been used and left virtually unchanged for the past fifteen years. At first glance, he thought the comment cards were small, dull, and cheaply printed, and it looked like they were heading for the cleaning crew's trash cart. It also struck him that the expression "O.K." kept coming up, when guests were asked to describe their stay at Ambassador Suites in their own words. O.K. is an expression Doug Saunders does not like, as he has been striving for excellence all his career. He wanted to determine exactly what factors drive guest satisfaction during their visits to Ambassador Suites, so that any changes he implemented would add to the customer-perceived value. He wanted to know how satisfaction evolves during a visit and what factors slow down and speed up the formation of guest satisfaction. Which components of the service delivery have a negative impact on satisfaction? How can high satisfaction levels be secured from the start?

In facing questions like these, he always remembers the comment made by one of the inventors of customer service excellence, Walt Disney, who said that "there is no magic to magic, it's all in the details!" So, the new COO of Ambassador Suites went looking for details. He decided to first design a new guest evaluation system that is as easy to administer as the familiar comment cards. The system looks at the customer value chain as consisting of a number of stages that hotel guests go through during a visit and relates these to satisfaction. Doug calls his system "the customer-perceived value approach to profiling satisfaction."

The Customer Value Approach

The customer-perceived value approach is based on two profiles that are important to a hotel visit:

1. A satisfaction profile at the general level
2. A value profile at the detailed level

A hotel visit can be viewed as a series of value-generating stages, all leading to the total customer-perceived value of the visit. It can be profiled in terms of a distinct number of stages. It includes check-in, room, restaurant, breakfast, and check-out. After completing each stage, guests are asked how satisfied they are so far with the number of stages they have gone through. In this way, a satisfaction profile of the hotel chain can be obtained.

Each stage contributes cumulatively to final overall satisfaction. The hotel visit is a chain of value-generating stages that is only as strong as its weakest link. With the help of a satisfaction profile, strong and weak links in the chain can be identified. Customer-perceived value ultimately determines satisfaction.

Having majored in marketing and philosophy, Doug has learned that the value concept consists of three underlying dimensions, namely, the emotional, the practical, and the logical. Of course, he realizes that these "deep thoughts" will not be easily digested by the Ambassador management team. Therefore, he uses what he calls a "guest route" as a concrete example to prove his point to them. He asks the team to picture a guest entering the hotel, ready to check-in. With regards to the check-in procedure the guest is expecting to be treated nicely and politely (the emotional dimension); he expects the clerk to perform his or her job efficiently so that he does not have to wait very long (the practical value dimension); and, he expects that his reservation has been processed correctly (the logical dimension). Next, the guest expects his room to be cozy (emotional), equipped with comfortable furniture (practical), and to obtain value-for-money (logical). After leaving his luggage in the room and a quick shower, the guest heads for the hotel restaurant where he will be looking for a fine atmosphere (emotional), good food (practical), and value-for-money (logical).

In this way each stage can be profiled comprehensively in terms of the same three dimensions. This yields a customer value profile, which is a detailed picture of each stage. Thus, with the help of the customer value approach a clear picture can be obtained of how satisfaction evolves during the service delivery process and which value factors are responsible for these fluctuations.

Data Collection

In order to test his new approach, Doug chose the Boston Ambassador Suites for a pretest, also called a "beta site." One hundred fifty randomly selected guests were invited to participate in a pilot project. The one selection criterion used was that they had to go through all five stages (this meant that they had to visit the restaurant and have breakfast at least once). Upon entering the hotel, guests are handed a little booklet containing little colored slips of paper, each referring to one stage in the visit. They are requested to answer the four questions, tear off one slip and put it in a specially designed letter box immediately after completion of each stage.

Figure 10–4.1 shows the various slips contained in the guest evaluation booklet. In order to expedite the data collection, an 11-point answering scale

Before filling in the questionnaire please read the following instructions carefully.

- Please answer each part of the questionnaire directly after the relevant stage.
- Answer each question on a scale from 1 to 11 (1 = strongly disagree, 6 = neutral, 11 = strongly agree).
- Please hand in your questionnaire at the reception after checking out and filling in the last questions.

Thank you for participating in this research.

GENERAL QUESTIONS

1. Nationality?   USA (. . .) GB (. . .) F (. . .) B (. . .) NL (. . .)
   Other (. . .) i.e.: . . . .
2. Gender?   Male (. . .)   Female (. . .)
3. Age?   <20 (. . .)   31–40 (. . .)   51–60 (. . .)
            21–30 (. . .)   41–50 (. . .)   > 61 (. . .)
4. Did you stay in this hotel before? Yes (. . .)   No (. . .)
5. What is the reason for your stay? Business (. . .) Pleasure (. . .)
   Meeting (. . .)

RESTAURANT

	☹									☺
1. Fine atmosphere?	1 2 3 4 5 6 7 8 9 10 11
2. Good food?	1 2 3 4 5 6 7 8 9 10 11
3. Value for money?	1 2 3 4 5 6 7 8 9 10 11
4. How satisfied are you now?	1 2 3 4 5 6 7 8 9 10 11

☹   ☺

Figure 10–4.1.   The customer value booklet.

BREAKFAST

☹   ☺

1. Calm atmosphere?   1 2 3 4 5 6 7 8 9 10 11
2. Abundant and easy to get food? 1 2 3 4 5 6 7 8 9 10 11
3. Good selection of food?   1 2 3 4 5 6 7 8 9 10 11

4. How satisfied are you now?   1 2 3 4 5 6 7 8 9 10 11

☹   ☺

CHECK-IN

☹   ☺

1. Nice treatment?   1 2 3 4 5 6 7 8 9 10 11
2. Quick check-in?   1 2 3 4 5 6 7 8 9 10 11
3. Correct booking?   1 2 3 4 5 6 7 8 9 10 11

4. How satisfied are you now?   1 2 3 4 5 6 7 8 9 10 11

☹   ☺

ROOM

☹   ☺

1. Cozy room?   1 2 3 4 5 6 7 8 9 10 11
2. Are furniture and equipment
   useful?   1 2 3 4 5 6 7 8 9 10 11
3. Value for money?   1 2 3 4 5 6 7 8 9 10 11

4. How satisfied are you now?   1 2 3 4 5 6 7 8 9 10 11

☹   ☺

Figure 10–4.1. Continued

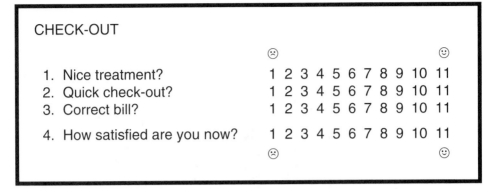

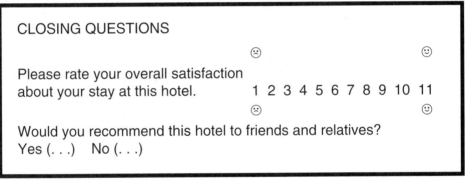

Figure 10–4.1. Continued

was used with short statements and faces at the ends of the scale so that quick and spontaneous reactions could be obtained.

The majority of the respondents in the sample are male (76%). Sixty percent of the respondents are between 31 and 50 years old. Most guests are repeat visitors—78 percent had stayed in the hotel before. Not surprisingly, the hotel is most frequently visited by business travellers (63%). Finally, 81 percent would recommend the hotel to friends and relatives.

Data Analysis

First, the average satisfaction scores per stage are calculated. The satisfaction profile is depicted in Figure 10–4.2. A clear trend emerges from the data, namely:

1. "Check-in" results in relatively high satisfaction
2. Satisfaction with the "Room" is lower
3. It gets worse as guests use the "Restaurant"

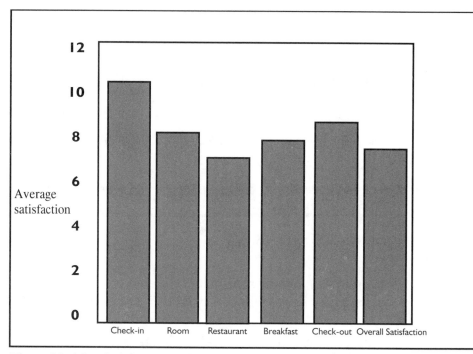

Figure 10–4.2.   Satisfaction profile.

4. Satisfaction scores go up again as "Breakfast" is ordered and rise even more after "Checking out"

Nevertheless, after all is said and done, the overall satisfaction is disappointing by Ambassador standards. Next, regression analysis, a technique that measures the relative strength of each (independent) variable in its relation to a dependent variable (overall satisfaction) is applied (see Chapter 4, Figures 4–11 and 4–12). Here's how Doug interprets the output. The results, shown in Table 10–4.1, indicate that the model has a high explanatory power as indicated by the R^2 of 0.61. It also becomes clear that breakfast and the room are the stages that have the highest impact on overall satisfaction. This is indicated by the Beta values in Table 10–4.1 (a Beta = 0 means there is no influence).

Oddly enough, the restaurant is not a significant element in determining overall satisfaction, see Table 10–4.1. Doug concludes this because the T value, the statistic that indicated whether there is a significant influence, is not significant at the 5 percent level.

On a more detailed level, the value profiles of each individual stage are calculated in order to obtain an insight into how satisfaction scores are made up. These are shown in Figure 10–4.3.

TABLE 10–4.1. Regression Analysis on Overall Satisfaction

Variables	Beta	t-value	Significance
Check-in	0.17	3.453	0.0006
Room	0.30	6.643	< 0.00001
Breakfast	0.24	4.773	< 0.00001
Restaurant	0.01	0.119	0.9054
Check-out	0.12	2.199	0.0287
Adjusted R^2 0.61			

The stage profiles render a detailed insight into guest evaluation of the individual stages. For the check-in stage all three dimensions are evaluated in a very positive manner. Especially, the emotional value ("nice treatment") dimension receives a high rating. The profiles for the room and breakfast are more or less the same, with the lowest ratings for the practical dimensions ("useful furniture"/"abundant and easy to get food"). The restaurant profile reveals that particularly the emotional and logical value dimensions ("atmosphere" and "value-for-money") are lagging behind.

From Data to Management Information

The results of the customer-perceived value approach yield very actionable results. There is considerable fluctuation in relation to customer satisfaction. In the beginning, friendly treatment by receptionists makes for a positive start. Satisfaction drops after the guest has entered the room and rises again when he or she has had breakfast. These two stages are nevertheless considered as the most important determinant of overall satisfaction. They make up the core of the hotel service, and therefore, quality improvements in these stages are likely to have the most positive impact on overall satisfaction (which is now relatively low).

Such improvements should focus primarily on the practical value dimension, where the restaurant receives the lowest ratings. Moreover, it does not contribute significantly to the overall judgment by hotel guests. One explanation for this is that guests do not view the restaurant as essential to the hotel service. Quality improvements regarding the restaurant should be directed primarily at the emotional and logical dimensions.

From Management Information to Action

The Ambassador management team is very pleased with the in-depth insight obtained by Doug's customer-perceived value approach to guest satisfaction. One of the first actions they undertake, therefore, is to order a company-wide

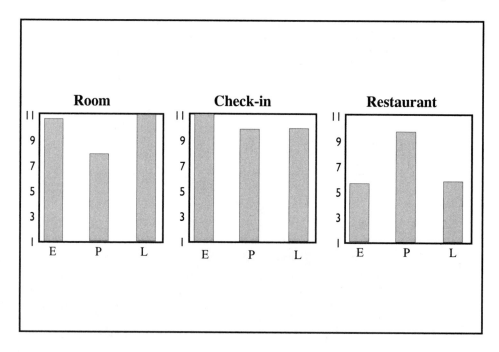

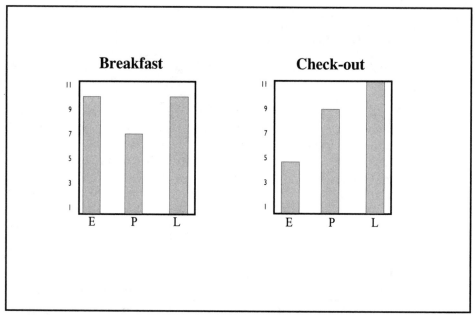

Figure 10–4.3. The value profiles.

implementation, replacing the old comment card system. In this way satisfaction can be monitored at each of the 67 hotels owned by Ambassador. Since the results of the pilot study are considered "very promising," it is decided to make the Boston hotel an ongoing beta site for quality improvement efforts and to use the results of this study as a baseline. These efforts are concentrated on the room and breakfast.

Also, the restaurant is included in the pilot in quality improvement. The management team considers it a vital element of the hotel service in order to be able to cater to conference guests, despite the fact that it does not contribute significantly to overall guest satisfaction. With regards to the room, the standard furniture and equipment is evaluated and a number of outdated items are replaced such as the hotel alarm clock. Likewise a number of items on the breakfast order list are replaced in order to improve the perceived quality of the food. For the restaurant a major redecoration is planned and training sessions on developing a customer-oriented attitude are organized for restaurant personnel.

LESSONS LEARNED

✔ The customer-perceived value approach offers an insight into the dynamics of satisfaction during the service delivery process.

✔ The customer-perceived value approach profiles the different stages in a detailed manner.

✔ The customer-perceived value approach clearly pinpoints quality improvement areas.

✔ The customer-perceived value approach is relatively inexpensive and easy-to-administer for monitoring satisfaction.

CASE 5 *The Perceived Dynamics of Service Quality*

Case Overview

A large moderately priced department store chain, called the Fashionating Store, specializes in national brands and quality private-labeled casual apparel. Presently, the company has 235 stores in 15 states, most of which are on the West Coast. Fashionating is a customer-focused company. Its mission statement is based on the following two principles:

1. "Selling isn't compelling, customer satisfaction is"
2. "Sales won't last, customer loyalty will"

Over the years Fashionating Store management has been closely monitoring customer relationships. The backbone of Fashionating customer research program forms the Customer Relationship Barometer, an extensive survey system, based on a panel of 12,000 Fashionating customers, that measures customer-perceived quality on a continual basis.

With the help of this high-frequency customer input, trends are easy to observe. Quality indices are calculated for individual department stores and fluctuations resulting from quality improvements and innovative actions emerge easily from the data. Lately, however, business has slowed down, and in the case of a number of stores, losses are seen for the first time in years.

In order to cope with these losses, a large-scale reorganization plan has been designed by the Board of Directors. The plan proposes a number of cutbacks, particularly with respect to activities of Fashionating's San Francisco headquarters. Marketing research, too, is facing budget restrictions. For this reason, the marketing research manager, Jennifer Boulding, has to discontinue the Barometer, simply because it is by far the largest item on her departmental budget. Besides, the Barometer system was showing response problems, for example, in 1993 when the fourth wave of questionnaires was sent out, only 36 percent of the panel members answered the questionnaires. However, when Jennifer announces her plans, a large number of store operations managers express their concern, saying that they need the information to stay close to their customers.

In response, The Board of Directors assigns Jennifer the task of developing a measurement instrument that yields information on the dynamics in customer-perceived value, and one that is more affordable and reliable than the panel-based Customer Relations Barometer. After consulting with her college professor, Dr. David Atwood, a marketing research specialist, Jennifer proposes to test a method which she calls the Perceived Dynamics Method (PDM).

PDM focuses on quality evaluations of the shopper's current visit to the store in relation to an assessment of all previous visits. The method is to be pretested in one of the company's San Francisco stores, which also had been the test site for a number of in-store innovations, such as new layout, a customer information desk and personnel training in customer service. Apart from testing PDM, the effect of these store innovations were also to be examined.

The Perceived Dynamics Method

The PDM invites respondents to reflect on the present visit (or episode) as well as make an overall assessment of the quality of previous visits which, in fact, constitute the shopper's relationship with a store. Relationship quality, as it were, is viewed as the sum of the perceived quality of all previous episodes. On the basis of a comparison between episode and relationship quality, an indication of the dynamics of perceived value can be obtained. PDM does not require the use of the same respondents. It can simply be used with a random sample of department store shoppers.

Data Collection

Questionnaires were administered by means of personal interviews conducted by two members of the marketing research staff. In total 499 customers visiting the beta site department store participated in the research. The sample only included customers that visited the stores at least three times in the previous three months. These customers were considered to have developed a relationship with the Fashionating Store. Customers were asked to indicate their opinion on the service quality of their current visit (i.e., the episode) as well as on the service quality of their previous visits to the store (i.e., their relationship).

The questionnaire was based on the one that was used for the Customer Relation Barometer, which in turn was based on the well-known SERVQUAL questionnaire style. This is a frequently used service quality measurement instrument comprising the five dimensions of service, namely tangibles, reliability, responsiveness, assurance and empathy, and was discussed in Chapters 6 and 7.

Episode and relationship performance were measured using fifteen service aspects on a 7-point scale. One item was added to the questionnaire assessing core service of the department store, that is, selling clothing items. In addition, a general (one-dimensional) measure pertaining to overall episode and relationship quality was added for the purpose of further analysis (see Table 10–5.1).

Data Analysis

The PDM includes some sophisticated quantitative analysis techniques in customer relationships. However, by using a PC-based data analysis software such as SPSS, data analysis can be performed with a few clicks of the mouse. In order to gain an insight into the extent of perceived dynamics, Ms. Boulding carries out a T-test in order to test for difference between the episode and the relationship level with regards to fifteen service attributes and core service. The T-test provides information on whether the degree of difference (with respect to the mean scores) between two data sets (in this case, episode versus relationship quality) is statistically significant.

Moreover, both factor analysis and subsequent regression analysis were conducted in order to determine differences between the episode and relationship level in the relationship with the one-dimensional measure of overall ser-

TABLE 10–5.1. Episode Performance versus Relationship Performance

Performance Attributes	Episode Level	Relationship Level
Tangibles		
(1) This store has a modern-looking interior.	5.47	4.35*
(2) This store is well organized.	4.98	3.95*
(3) Store personnel are neatly and well dressed.	5.82	4.88*
Reliability		
(4) Store personnel can be easily recognized.	4.52	4.79*
(5) This store always lives up to its promises.	5.02	4.88
(6) This store handles my payments at the cash register correctly and without errors.	6.44	6.13*
Responsiveness		
(7) Store personnel are always willing to help me.	5.58	3.60*
(8) Store personnel behavior instills confidence in me.	5.25	5.02*
Assurance		
(9) Store personnel are never too busy to help me.	5.29	5.30
(10) Store personnel are polite and friendly.	5.64	3.59*
(11) Store personnel are knowledgeable enough to answer all my questions.	4.90	3.91*
Empathy		
(12) The opening hours of this store are acceptable to me.	6.06	6.04
(13) Store personnel show a personal interest in me.	5.22	5.11
(14) This store makes a customer-oriented impression on me.	5.64	3.45*
(15) Store personnel understand my needs and wants.	5.18	4.18*
Core Service		
(16) This store served me well.	5.57	5.32*

* $p < 0.05$

vice quality as a dependent variable. Factor analysis is used to reduce the number of variables (in our case, the 15 + 1 service aspects), while regression analysis measures the relative strength of the relationship between variables (in our case, which variable most strongly influences overall shopper perception of service quality?).

From Data to Management Information

Table 10–5.1 presents the results of a *T*-test that was carried out in order to determine differences between episode and relationship service quality evaluations.

Statistically significant differences between the episode and relationship levels occur with respect to twelve out of sixteen service quality attributes.

The results show that the majority of attributes, as well as the core service, are rated significantly higher at the episode level. The dynamics in service quality clearly show the effect of the innovative program implemented at this Fashionating Store.

Subsequently, Ms. Boulding carries out a factor analysis on the service attributes to look for underlying patterns in the data. Factor analysis can be used to reduce the large number of service quality attributes to more manageable proportions. Tables 10–5.2 and 10–5.3 present the results of factor analysis on both the episode and the relationship level.

Two underlying factors (i.e., groups of attributes) can be identified on the basis of the results: *personnel controllable* and *management controllable*. Personnel controllable service attributes include responsiveness, assurance, and empathy. They relate to actual behavior of individual store personnel. The second factor, management controllable, comprises such attributes as living up to promises, recognizability and hours of operation, and tangible aspects. They relate primarily to aspects that typically fall under the responsibility of management.

Subsequently, multiple regression analysis on the two-factor solution, as well as the core (i.e., technical) service with overall service quality as the dependent variable on both levels is performed. Regression analysis is used to identify which factor(s) can be considered to be most influential in determining service quality. These can be identified by comparing the Beta scores, namely, the higher this score, the stronger the relationship. In Tables 10–5.4 and 10–5.5 the results are presented.

Reviewing Table 10–5.4, Jennifer concludes that at the service episode level, the factor management controllable attributes is most strongly related to overall service quality. This variable has the highest Beta score and is the only significant variable of the three. A completely different picture, however, emerges from Table 10–5.5. While both factors are statistically significant at

TABLE 10–5.2. **Factor Analysis of Episode Performance Attributes[a]**

No.	Performance Attributes	Factor Loadings[b]
	Factor 1: Personnel Controllable (Cronbach's α = 0.83)	
(9)	Store personnel are never too busy to help me.	0.79689
(7)	Store personnel are always willing to help me.	0.78013
(15)	Store personnel understand my needs and wants.	0.68801
(13)	Store personnel show a personal interest in me.	0.68550
(10)	Store personnel are polite and friendly.	0.67758
(8)	Store personnel behavior instills confidence in me.	0.65957
(11)	Store personnel are knowledgeable enough to answer all my questions.	0.62018
(14)	This store makes a customer-oriented impression on me.	0.57272
(1)	This store has a modern-looking interior.	0.44121
(3)	Store personnel are neatly and well dressed.	0.42474
(6)	The store handles my payments at the cash register correctly and without errors.	—
	Factor 2: Management Controllable (Cronbach's α = 0.48)	
(5)	This store always lives up to its promises.	0.80269
(4)	Store personnel can be easily recognized.	0.74625
(12)	The opening hours of the store are acceptable to me.	0.43039
(2)	This store is well organized.	—
	Total Explained Variance	*40.9%*

[a]Principal Components Factor Analysis and Varimax Rotation
[b]Factor Loadings > 0.4

the relationship level, the personnel controllable performance factor has the highest Beta score and thus yields the strongest relationship with overall service quality.

The results clearly show the effect of the store's innovative programs. Aspects related to management control are the strongest determinant of service quality of the present visit. In her memo to the Board, Jennifer also concludes that in regard to customer relationship management personnel attitude and behavior are especially important, so that personnel training in customer service

TABLE 10–5.3. Factor Analysis of Relationship Performance Attributes[a]

No.	Performance Attributes	Factor Loadings[b]
Factor 1: Personnel Controllable (Cronbach's α = 0.83)		
(10)	Store personnel are polite and friendly.	0.79296
(7)	Store personnel are always willing to help me.	0.77367
(9)	Store personnel are never too busy to help me.	0.73922
(8)	Store personnel behavior instills confidence in me.	0.70866
(13)	Store personnel show a personal interest in me.	0.70585
(15)	Store personnel understand my needs and wants.	0.70365
(14)	This store makes a customer-oriented impression on me.	0.69646
(11)	Store personnel are knowledgeable enough to answer all my questions.	0.58503
(2)	This store is well organized.	0.43124
(1)	This store has a modern-looking interior.	—
Factor 2: Management Controllable (Cronbach's α = 0.50)		
(4)	Store personnel can be easily recognized.	0.68387
(5)	This store always lives up to its promises.	0.60423
(12)	The opening hours of the store are acceptable to me.	0.56809
(3)	Store personnel are neatly and well drssed.	0.52450
(6)	The store handles my payments at the cash register correctly and without errors.	0.50513
Total Explained Variance		*43.0%*

[a]Principal Components Factor Analysis and Varimax Rotation
[b]Factor Loadings > 0.4

TABLE 10–5.4. Regression Analysis on Episode Service Quality

Variables		Beta	t-value	Significance
Factor 1: Personnel Controllable		0.1079	1.532	0.1269
Factor 2: Management Controllable		0.2668	4.319	< 0.00001
Core service		0.1724	2.363	0.0189
Adjusted R^2	0.15			

TABLE 10–5.5. **Regression Analysis on Relationship Service Quality**

Variables		Beta	t-value	Significance
Factor 1: Personnel Controllable		0.4256	6.087	< 0.00001
Factor 2: Management Controllable		0.1518	2.582	0.0104
Core service		0.0404	0.560	0.5760
Adjusted R^2	0.22			

should definitely be included in the program, in addition to in-store information desks, and store layout innovations.

From Management Information to Action

The Board of Directors of the Fashionating Store chain is pleased with the results of the pretest of the PDM. They realize that customer perception is reality for them. If customers perceive a difference between the present visit and all previous visits to the Fashionating Store, then this is clearly an indication of the fact that service quality is a moving target. Customers will adjust their perceptions taking both previous visits and the present visit into account. They will always ask "What have you done for me lately?" Therefore, it is decided to continue both the application of the PDM, as well as further testing of the PDM in a larger number of stores. In case of the San Francisco beta site, the difference between episode and relationship was positive for all service attributes.

The Board realizes that a negative trend in management controllable attributes is also occurring. It is decided that if a negative trend is encountered more than once at a given store, a so-called *Dissatisfaction Bust Team* will be sent in and not leave the premises until a positive trend in the differences between episode and relationship quality emerges from the PDM. The *Dissatisfaction Bust Team* is a group of internal consultants and trainers specializing in customer satisfaction. They will analyze the data pertaining to a particular store in detail and implement a number of quality improvement measures.

LESSONS LEARNED

✔ The PDM acknowledges that service quality is a transitory phenomenon that is subject to fluctuations over time.

✔ The PDM quantifies the impact of service quality improvement and innovation efforts.

✔ The PDM is a relatively easy-to-administer instrument for monitoring service quality.

✔ The PDM is an affordable alternative to the use of longitudinal panel data for customer relationship management.

Fuzzy Logic Listing

Fuzzy Logic 1.1   *"The key is getting closer to our customers and making it easier for them to do business with us."*

Fuzzy Logic 1.2   *"Modern information technology makes possible these close, 'customerized' relationships that lock in customers for life by substantially enhancing the customer-perceived value of the product/service."*

Fuzzy Logic 1.3   *"Be careful not to use information technology to simply 'pave the cow paths' of traditional business processes that affect customer relationships."*

Fuzzy Logic 1.4   *"First let's get effective, then let's get efficient."*

Fuzzy Logic 1.5   *"Across a wide range of business, the pattern is the same: The longer a company keeps a customer, the more money it stands to make."*

Fuzzy Logic 2.1   *"Only measure what you plan to improve."*

Fuzzy Logic 2.2   *"In order to include the voice of the customer in our management style, we must include measurements that are indicative of customer satisfaction."*

Fuzzy Logic 2.3   *"Loyal customers expect a good price, but they crave value most of all."*

Fuzzy Logic 2.4   *"The company with the most information wins!"*

Fuzzy Logic 2.5   *"Customer satisfaction is a state of mind in which his or her needs, wants, and expectations throughout the product/service life have been meet or exceeded, resulting in repurchase and loyalty."*

Fuzzy Logic 2.6   *"Satisfied customers will (a) repurchase your products/ser-*

vices, (b) recommend your products/services to others, and (c) generate positive word of mouth."

Fuzzy Logic 2.7 "The customer, of course, is always right."

Fuzzy Logic 2.8 "Positive word of mouth will not necessarily get you the sale, however, negative word of mouth essentially guarantees you will not get the sale."

Fuzzy Logic 2.9 "A moment of truth is defined as every opportunity that the customer has to experience and evaluate his or her relationship with your company."

Fuzzy Logic 2.10 "A delighted customer is six times more likely to repurchase your product or service than a satisfied customer."

Fuzzy Logic 3.1 "Qualitative measurement probes the environment surrounding an observed phenomenon."

Fuzzy Logic 3.2 "It is not only unwise, but potentially dangerous, to make major changes in customer relationship management policy based solely on a qualitative study."

Fuzzy Logic 4.1 "You cannot improve externally what you don't measure internally."

Fuzzy Logic 4.2 "Where possible, you should ensure that the internal metrics that you select are behaviorally anchored."

Fuzzy Logic 4.3 "Today's busy and cost-conscious customers focus almost exclusively on value."

Fuzzy Logic 4.4 "Customers switch suppliers because they are not satisfied with the company's perceived value, relative to the competition."

Fuzzy Logic 4.5 "The proper goal is to achieve superior customer relationship value in areas that matter to the customer, together with a cost structure no higher than that of lower quality competitors."

Fuzzy Logic 4.6 "The better soft data is presented to management, the greater the likelihood action will be taken."

Fuzzy Logic 6.1 "Target customers will have very specific expectations before experiencing each of the above company processes, and they will acquire specific perceptions as they use your customer service strategy."

Fuzzy Logic 9.1 "Let the customer decide for you."

Fuzzy Logic 9.2 "Let the customer define the outcome of each of your company's processes."

Fuzzy Logic 9.3 "When the customer is invited to advise you on how to operate your business, you are rewarded by positive referrals and product loyalty."

Fuzzy Logic 9.4   *"Service is the link between the producer and customers, both internal and external."*

Fuzzy Logic 9.5   *"In today's business world, to retain customers you cannot look at it as if you were selling a product, instead, you are providing customer-perceived value."*

Fuzzy Logic 9.6   *"Let's not forget that the customer is the only reason for our business."*

References

Anton, J. (May 1994). *Internal research report.* W. Lafayette, IN: Purdue University Center for Customer-Driven Quality.

Anton, J., Bennett, R., & Widdows, R. (1994). *Call-center design and implementation.* Houston, TX: Dame Publications.

Anton, J., & de Ruyter, J.C. (Fall 1991). Van Klachten naar Managementinformatie. *Harvard Holland Review, 27.*

Berry, L.L. (April 1988). Delivering excellent service in retailing. *Arthur Andersen Retailing Issues Letter.*

Berry, L.L., & Parasuraman, A. (1991). *Marketing services.* New York: The Free Press.

Betts, M. (March 1993). Real IS payoff lies in business benefits. *Computerworld, 56.*

Clark, T. (July 1993). Marketing key to HP's battle plan. *Business Marketing, 15.*

Clemmer, J. (Winter 1993). Making change work: Integrating focus, effort, and direction. *Canadian Business Review, 30.*

Cronin, J.J., & Taylor, S.A. (July 1992). Measuring service quality. *Journal of Marketing, 56.*

Davidow, W.H., & Uttal, B. (1989). *Total customer service.* New York: Harper & Row.

Davis, T.R.V. (January/February 1992). Satisfying internal customers: The link to external customer satisfaction. *Planning Review,* 35.

Drucker, P. F. (1979). *Adventures of a bystander.* New York: Harper & Row.

Dutka, A. (1993). *AMA handbook for customer satisfaction.* Lincolnwood, IL: NTC Publishing Group.

Ernst & Young Survey. (March 1990). Biggest challenge for next five years. *Electronic Business Magazine,* 33.

Feinberg, R., & Widdows, R. (n.d.). The critical incident technique. *Mobius,* 8.2, 8.

Freedman, D.H. (August 1993). A model worth copying. *CIO Magazine,* 42.

Gale, B.T. (July/August 1992). Relative perceived quality. *Planning Review,* 7.

Hamilton-Smith, K., & Morris, T. (May 1993) Market-driven quality. *CMA Magazine,* 24.

Harris, A.S. (June 1991). The customer's always right. *Black Enterprise,* 234.

Hughes, D.H. (November 1992). We can't get there from here. *CMA Magazine,* 12.

Knauer, V. (1992). *Increasing customer satisfaction.* Pueblo, CO: United States Office of Consumer Affairs.

Lawton, L. (September 1991). Creating a customer-centered culture in service industries. *Quality Process,* 71.

Lian, T. (February 1994). Helping hands. *Bank Marketing,* 25.

Mackay, H. (1993) *Swim with the sharks without being eaten alive.* New York: William Morrow & Company.

Mather, H.F. (March/April 1993). Do more than just satisfy your customers—profitably delight them. *Industrial Marketing,* 11.

McGarvey, R. (July 1995). The big thrill. *Entrepreneur,* 86.

Panepinto, J. (February 1994). Going out on a wireless. *Computerworld,* 99.

Plymire, J. (March/April 1991). Complaints as opportunities. *Business Horizons,* 80.

Reichheld, F.F. (March-April 1993). Loyalty-based management. *Harvard Business Review,* 65.

Reichheld, F.F., & Sasser, W.E. Jr. (September/October 1990). Zero defects: Quality comes to services. *Harvard Business Review*, 106.

Rust, R.T., Zahorik, A.J., & Keiningham, T.L. (1994). *Return on quality.* Chicago: Probus Publishing Company.

Sager, I. (May 30, 1994). The few, the true, the blue. *Business Week*, 124.

Shetty, Y.K. (Spring 1993). The quest for quality excellence: Lessons from the Malcolm Baldridge Quality Award. *Advanced Management Journal*, 37.

Shrednick, H.R. (January 30, 1995). A decade of improvements. *Information Week*, 112.

Shycon, H.N. (January/February 1992). Improving customer service: Measuring the payoff. *Journal of Business Strategy*, 15.

Spector, P.E. (n.d.). *Summated rating scale construction: An introduction paper series on quantitative applications in the social sciences*, Series Number 07-082. Newbury Park, CA: Sage University.

Tanaka, J. (October 1991). Going for the glory. *Business Week*, 60.

Tehrani, N. (March 1993). Customer service & inbound telemarketing . . . The new powerful way to expand market share. *Telemarketing*, 76.

Tschohl, J. (June 1993). For service that sells, you need service strategy. *Chain Store Age Executive*, 60.

Williamson, M. (August 1993). Golden handcuffs. *CIO*, 48, 49.

Zeithaml, V., Parasuraman, A., & Berry, L.L. (1990). *Delivering quality service*. New York: The Free Press.

Index